Women's
Retreats

Women's
Retreats

A Creative Planning Guide

Sue Edwards | Kelley Mathews | Linda Robinson
Mechelle Larson, illustrator

Kregel
Publications

Women's Retreats: A Creative Planning Guide

© 2004 by Sue Edwards, Kelley Mathews, and Linda Robinson
Illustrations © 2004 by Mechelle Larson

Published by Kregel Publications, a division of Kregel, Inc., P.O. Box 2607, Grand Rapids, MI 49501.

Library of Congress Cataloging-in-Publication Data
Edwards, Sue.
    Women's retreats: a creative planning guide / by Sue Edwards, Kelley Mathews & Linda Robinson.
        p. cm.
Includes bibliographical references.
    1. Spiritual retreats for women. 2. Women—Religious life.
I. Mathews, Kelley. II. Robinson, Linda. III. Title.
BV5068.R4E36   2004
269.6'43—dc22   2004013943

Cover design: John M. Lucas

ISBN 0-8254-2507-7

Printed in the United States of America

04 05 06 07 08 / 5 4 3 2 1

To our husbands—
David Edwards, John Mathews, and John Robinson—
for a combined seventy years of love, devotion, and support
(with just enough spice to keep life interesting).
We're looking forward to the next seventy!

Contents

Preface

*I*f you are a women's director seeking a quality weekend of spiritual, emotional, and physical refreshment for the women in your church, then this book is for you. It is our hope that this manual will serve as a helpful counselor as you journey through the planning stages of your women's retreat. We also encourage you to take it along to your retreat planning meetings and use it in discipling and training the members of your retreat team.

Part one will take you, step by step, through the preparation and planning process. Part two brings it all alive with five proven, successful programs. You will find retreat ideas for churches big and small—feel free to change them to fit your particular needs. Have fun with it, and give it your all.

The art and appendices were included specifically to give real-life examples of the dynamic process of creating an effective, life-changing women's retreat. Additional resources for women's ministry can be found on our Web site, www.newdoors.info. We can be contacted through our Web site as well. We welcome your questions and comments.

Acknowledgments

*O*ne of them, when he saw he was healed, came back, praising God in a loud voice" (Luke 17:15). Words seem small when we attempt to thank God for His tender mercies and goodness, for family and friends, and for strength and ministry opportunities. You, Lord, are our deepest Love; life with You is an amazing journey!

Thanks to Pat Knight, who birthed the process over twenty-five years ago; Karen Black, who graciously shared her outstanding scripts; Mary Bodien, for her contributions to our worship material; and other women on the Irving Baptist Church (IBC) retreat team, whose diligent labor of love helped make these sample retreats reality.

Sue especially thanks Dr. Mike Lawson, who leads the Dallas Theological Seminary Christian Education department with a fierce passion to prepare men and women for life-transforming ministry. As he supports his team with a godly father's devotion, his enthusiasm is contagious. I am grateful for the opportunity to serve alongside the devoted men and women who comprise the CE staff. I also want to express a special appreciation to Joye Baker, my dear friend and cotraveler on this new academic adventure.

Preparation and Process

*I*t's time for a retreat! Many times all we know is that we want to get away, and the *why* and the *how* escape us. The first part of the manual will guide the women's director and retreat coordinator down the detailed path of producing a top-notch retreat. We'll examine the reasons for even having a retreat, the kinds of women you'll be trying to reach through it, and the defining characteristics that suit each member to particular roles on the planning team.

Once you define your motive and form your team, the work has only just begun. Where will you go, when will you go, how will you get from here to there? We'll point you toward the answers to these and many more questions in the pages ahead, helping you catch even the small details that often get overlooked. We'll also share some helpful hints for working with retreat centers and their representatives and give you a timeline to help you check your planning progress, taking you step-by-step through the months preceding your retreat.

A well-planned retreat will provide spiritual, emotional, and physical refreshment, but the good news is that the planning itself may turn out to be an unforeseen bonus. It has been our experience that the process provides numerous opportunities to encourage, exhort, and disciple one another while you work as a unified band of willing women to make the retreat weekend the most memorable one of the year. We trust you will find your experience to be the same.

And now, without further ado . . . let the planning begin!

Chapter 1

Define Your Purpose

Why Retreat?

Be still, and know that I am God. (Psalm 46:10)

How often are you still? How often do you stop your daily routine, putting down your to-do list to focus on knowing God? How often do you assess the direction of your life and relationships? Remember, according to Socrates, "The unexamined life is not worth living." But the pace of new-millennium life chokes stillness and self-examination. How can we know God if we seldom stop to look at Him? How can our lives be balanced and joyful if we seldom stop to take account? Women's ministries that transform lives plan periodic times away for women to be still, to draw closer to their Creator and to each other. We call these days away *retreats*. To "retreat" means to draw back to a place of refuge, privacy, or safety, sometimes to escape danger or difficulty.

A retreat will offer a place where women have an opportunity to share their lives with one another, as Paul did when he told the Thessalonians, "We are determined to share with you not only the gospel of God but also our own selves" (1 Thess. 2:8 NRSV). Yes, the gospel of Christ is shared—believing women have the chance to model, perhaps even discuss, their faith with visiting friends and nonbelievers who attend. And a retreat allows women to open their hearts to new friends, inviting them to enjoy a unique camaraderie.

An American Custom

Build a community Most evangelical churches in America sponsor an annual retreat for women. Women who feel part of the community look forward to spending several days relaxing with friends and hearing an inspirational speaker. Confident newcomers see the retreat as an opportunity to plug into a new church home. But women on the fringes, seekers, and nonbelievers are often reluctant to spend several days with people they don't know well. They aren't sure they will be comfortable talking about "spiritual things." You may hear them use excuses such as "I'm not a retreat person."

How do we woo them to join us? How do we ensure that the "old timers" will reach out and embrace the newcomers? How do we set the stage for life transformation and "fork-in-the-road" decisions? How do we create an authentic atmosphere of relaxation and fun while focusing on the major purpose—an encounter with the living God? We wrote this book to answer these and other related questions.

Who Are We and What Qualifies Us to Write a Book on Retreats?

For six years, Sue led the women's ministry at Irving Bible Church, a growing megachurch in the Dallas area. She has worked with retreat teams and observed and spoken at a variety of retreats for over twenty-five years. On her team, Linda heads up the annual retreat committee and works throughout the year with other churches to help them birth exciting, impacting retreats. Linda has seen retreats at IBC grow from thirty women in 1981 to more than six hundred in 2004. She knows how to plan for twenty, one hundred, or seven hundred attendees. Kelley oversees the women's ministry at Creekside Bible Fellowship, also in the Dallas area, and will provide insight on retreats in small church settings. In addition, *New Doors in Ministry to Women*[1], by Sue and Kelley, provides helpful models for creating and growing a transformational women's ministry. Feel free to contact us on our Web site, www. newdoors.info, with your comments, questions, and creative ideas that have worked for you.

Just as important as our experience is the passion we share to produce retreats that transform the lives of women—both those who work on the retreat and those who attend it. Women today won't come back to retreats that are sloppily organized, cliquish, shallow, and stilted.

Both Linda Robinson (retreat consultant) and Karen Black (scriptwriter) are available to consult with you and your retreat committee regarding your future retreat plans. Over the years they have gone into other churches and organized retreats for them, modeling how to coordinate them. They have also worked with retreat committees to help them capture the vision. They consider it a privilege to help other women's ministries launch their retreats. Please feel free to contact either Linda at lrobinson@kregel.com or Karen at kblack@kregel.com.

We'll show you how to unleash the creative gifts of women who make life-size decorations, write and act in dramas, create worship that complements the teaching and theme, lead connecting groups, and participate in a plethora of other ministry opportunities. We'll give you a timetable to help you avoid last-minute hassles and conflict. We'll give pointers on recruiting volunteers, staying within a budget, picking a place and negotiating contracts, and choosing the right speaker. As you delegate the details, you'll enlist an army to share the joy of blessing women now and for eternity. And we'll even show you how to train your attendees to open their arms and set a welcome atmosphere for all.

Show, Don't Tell

Possibly the most helpful section of this book is part 2. Here we present five actual retreats with "how to" instructions for programming, sets, decorations, drama, and games. We'll help you market these retreat themes to attract your women without giving away the surprises that are revealed once they arrive. You can tweak these ideas to fit your size, setting, and budget. We'll include instructions for large and small groups.

Who's Coming?

Women's retreats are usually open to all the women of the church. Women today lead different lives from the sixties homemakers with 2.2 children. Almost 70 percent of Christian women work outside the home either full- or part-time, including almost 40 percent of mothers with preschool children. Thirty-six percent of women are single.[2] A healthy women's ministry attempts to help women know and enjoy each other, even at different ages and stages. In addition, women often like to invite friends, family, or coworkers, and sometimes these guests are unchurched, and even hostile, to faith. Women come with different agendas, perspectives, and expectations. Our challenge is to minister to them all—and we can!

The Nonbeliever

Women in the church are encouraged to invite their unbelieving friends to their retreat. They know that these friends and other visitors will be exposed to a community of real Christians. Such an experience will help break down stereotypes and introduce Jesus to them in a nonthreatening way. For many postmodern women, an "in your face" kind of evangelism is counterproductive. They are the "Oprah generation," many seeking spiritual alternatives and buying into radical feminism. But living in the midst of authentic community for several days is a powerful tool to reveal the true Christ and cause women to reflect on God, their lives, and choices.

The Stressed-out Woman

"It is estimated that seventy percent of all physician office visits are for stress-related illnesses. Workers in the United States consume fifteen tons of aspirin every day," writes counselor Dr. Elizabeth Baker.[3] Stress haunts every woman to some degree, and many do not know how to effectively fight it. A full forty-eight hours or more, away from everyday struggles and schedules, relaxing and communing with God, can be just what the doctor ordered. Why is extended time away so critical? Our health, both physical and spiritual, sometimes depends on it.

"It is not stress in itself that damages us, but *unrelenting* stress. . . . It is our failure to regularly retreat from the front lines that creates trouble. Observing our normal routine and planning times of retreat between peak stress times can help us recharge and prevent damage before it begins."[4] A women's retreat is one way to help women who need prolonged mental and spiritual rest. It provides solitude, time meditating on God and His works, unscheduled hours for naps, games, reading, and moments to share with friends. "We must leave the rat race to the rats. Instead, we carve out times of rest for our bodies and practice times of peace for our souls."[5]

allows women to retreat from the real world

The Newcomer

Millions of Americans relocate each year. For Christians that means leaving behind a history and finding a new church, acclimating to a new community where no one knows them, their gifts, or ministry experience. It takes time to feel at home and discover new friends. A retreat can jumpstart the adjustment. But we must be intentional in making newcomers feel welcome and comfortable. It won't happen unless we plan carefully and train women to reach out.

The Woman in Crisis

Shattered marriages, abuse, layoffs, runaway teens, cancer, infertility—there are hundreds of circumstances that afflict women today. Where can they go for healing, direction, and the energy to persevere? Several days with a group of supportive women that points to an ongoing, intimate relationship with Jesus can make all the difference.

The Fence-Sitter

It's easy to live with one foot in the church and one foot in the world. Pew warmers come and sit Sunday after Sunday without unmasking, connecting, or serving. They live with their boyfriends and steal from their bosses. They know their lifestyle choices don't mesh with what the preacher says, but they ignore what they don't want to hear. They want Jesus and they want their lives to change, but often they don't know how, and, of course, they resist changing what the flesh enjoys. The Holy Spirit can use a retreat setting to break through resistance. A block of time in the midst of committed women, hearing biblical, convicting messages from a gifted speaker can get women off the fence and change the direction of their lives.

The Outcast

A healthy church welcomes women of different races and economic backgrounds. Women raised in poverty and abuse often feel estranged from women who have never gone hungry or hidden in the closet from a drunken or drugged family member. A lovely Hispanic woman in our church wondered whether she would be accepted when the women learned of her former career—stripping in a local nightclub and prostitution. She had left that life behind and was working hard to overcome past sexual abuse that made her childhood a nightmare. Sobs of relief punctuated her testimony when she finally realized she was forgiven by God and embraced by her sisters. Create an atmosphere where women can find forgiveness at the retreat and change the life of the outcast forever.

The Wallflower

God has given the women in your church all the gifts required for a transforming women's ministry. But in some churches, those gifts lie dormant—tragically, sometimes forever. Women remain on the sidelines, fearful of getting involved. However, to enjoy the abundant Christian life, they must get into the dance. They must identify and develop those gifts, and you can help. A women's retreat is a time to investigate and discover those gifts because the fun-filled atmosphere tends to lessen inhibitions and fears. Women who would never sing, dance, or participate in a skit in a more formal church setting may give it a try at a retreat. Women who are afraid of making a long-term commitment will help out with the short-term involvement at a retreat. They know if they don't like it, they can easily say no next year. Wallflowers are often discovered at retreats and enter into a fuller experience in the life of the church from then on.

The Potential Leader

Retreats are a great training ground for future leaders. If a woman serves faithfully making name tags, you can see how she handles registration the next year. With so many new women coming into our churches each year, the retreat offers a place for women leaders to watch for future team captains and ministry managers. If your ministry is led by a lay board or team, you can observe workers that you may want to recruit to head up ministries later.

How Does a Retreat Change Lives?

Women attend retreats with certain expectations. What will they learn, who will they meet, how much sleep can they catch up on (or lose)? A transforming retreat will focus on three things:

1. *The Truths of Scripture:* However your retreat is organized, there should be solid teaching from the Word. A keynote speaker, workshops, small group discussions—any and all of these can teach scriptural principles and truths.
2. *Worship:* A good retreat will facilitate an atmosphere of worship—in song, prayer, meditation, and study. We'll give you some tips on how to help your women truly worship.
3. *Fun:* Let the women relax! We'll show you how to be highly organized without being overbearing and overscheduled. Give the women opportunities for free time as well as organized fun activities.

Note: A Retreat Is *Not* . . .

Let us take this moment to affirm that a quality women's retreat is *not* a forum for excessive emotion, a means to evoke strong sentimental reactions. Such "mountain high" experiences, we have learned, provide temporary euphoria but are actually exhausting, unrefreshing, and never truly relaxing. Women are emotional creatures, and we do expect some tears to flow at times, but we do not plan events in order to create such an emotional memory. Better to let God's Word touch their hearts in a permanent way.

Wendi's Experience

Wendi was a successful lawyer, but her evenings were increasingly spent in front of a big screen TV with a rum and coke—make that rum and cokes. Her husband of six years had encouraged her to take the promotion and move from their New England home to Dallas. His salary as an auto mechanic was a fraction of hers, but he liked his work and decided to stay until she was sure she liked her new job. The spark was flickering away.

The new job was challenging, but internal conflict in the firm made the days tense. Wendi wondered why there was so much competition. Weekends she worked at home or sat on the couch missing her cat, Honey. *I'll send for her soon,* Wendi thought.

Her neighbors Bonnie and Phil helped her hang a ceiling fan and made her a pie the day she moved in—a coconut cream pie. "Best pie I've had in years," she told Bonnie, and it was true. The homemade pie surprised Wendi because she didn't think anyone baked anymore. Nevertheless, the sense of being mothered lingered for months.

"A retreat—what's a retreat?" Wendi asked in response to Bonnie's invitation. "This one's just for women," explained Bonnie. "We get out of the city and into nature and just kick back for a couple days. You can ride horses, water ski, sing karaoke, or just relax with a good book. It would give you a chance to meet my friends. And we have a great speaker. I've heard her before. I'd love it if you'd come with me."

"I'll think about it," replied Wendi. She checked her calendar for that weekend. As usual, nothing. She liked Bonnie—a little weird, but genuine. "What could it hurt? I'll take my own car so I can escape if necessary," Wendi decided.

Wendi arrived late, but Bonnie had been watching for her. At check-in she received a cloth-quilted name tag and a tote bag loaded with folders and goodies like earplugs, lotion, and chocolate. On the tote bag were the words "Patterns of Our Lives." Wendi paused for a moment to think. "What's the pattern of my life? No, I'm not here to think. I'm here to relax."

The registration room fed into a huge room full of chairs—maybe four hundred. Around the walls hung dozens of quilts, and next to each quilt hung the story of the quilt and of the woman whose hands had delicately stitched each piece of fabric to make a beautiful whole. Interwoven in the words were legacies of wise women devoted to family, friends, and faith. Their stories intrigued Wendi.

She soon moved off to the dining hall to meet Bonnie's friends and was immersed in introductions, smiles, and laughter. Wendi was so engrossed in their interaction that she forgot the bland cafeteria food. She noticed a few other women like herself sitting in silence observing others, but most were caught up in stories and fun. Faint memories of Christy, her childhood friend, came to mind, and Wendi recalled that they used to laugh like that. She wondered what happened.

Four hundred women streamed into the quilt room, flopping down on red, yellow, or blue chair cushions. The first third of the room was red; the middle, yellow; and the back, blue. Wendi and Bonnie found two blue cushions. Being late had a price. But Linda, the emcee, introduced herself and asked each woman to sit on a different colored cushion each session. Wendi was glad for this instruction and hoped she would get to sit closer tomorrow.

In the middle of Linda's announcements, Rachmaninoff's "Flight of the Bumblebees" filled the room, and four women in brightly colored bumblebee suits buzzed out of a twelve-foot hive on the stage. Linda pretended to be surprised. They introduced themselves as Queen Bee, Quilting Bee, Spelling Bee, and Busy Bee.

Queen Bee was obviously the leader. After a few minutes of clever slapstick humor, the four buzzed off down the aisle to the roar of laughter. Their antics were silly, yet Wendi had to admit that the program was clever.

Linda introduced the worship leader and the speaker—both women belonged to Bonnie's church. Wendi wondered what church was like. She had never been in a church except for weddings and her grandfather's funeral.

Worship was an experience. Four hundred voices filled the room with praise. Bonnie showed her the words to the songs in her folder, and she joined in as best she could. Why were these women singing with such intensity? Soon she too was lost in melody and rhythm. But who was this God they were praising?

The speaker, Jackie, opened with a prayer that sounded like a conversation—no big words, no flowery language—just simple affection. For the next forty-five minutes, Wendi listened to her describe a sacred romance between herself and God.

She was introduced to Christ in her twenties by her fiancé, and they both had decided to follow Him. Within two years, they wearied of the corporate lifestyle and a marriage already on the rocks, so they left their jobs and traveled in a van for six months to focus on what God wanted for their lives.

They ended up in seminary, and now fifteen years later she was a Bible teacher. Jackie spoke of a new joy and a transformed life. Wendi marveled at how well she could relate to her experience: *Did they orchestrate this just for me? No, of course not. There are four hundred women in this room. Still . . .*

The women split up into small groups all over the camp. Bonnie and Wendi were in the same group, but everyone else was a stranger. They spent half an hour getting to know one another—two moms, a grandmother, three single women—one a paralegal.

Wendi connected with the paralegal, Susan, immediately. Although Susan worked for a law firm downtown and Wendi's firm was north of the city, her apartment was close to Wendi's rented house. Susan and Wendi talked for an hour after the small group while Bonnie visited with friends.

At the end of small group time, their leader gave each one a T-shirt that fit each woman perfectly with the same "Patterns of Life" logo as on her tote.

The rest of the day included snacks, games, loud music, karaoke in the barn, and talking into the night. Wendi and Bonnie sat on their beds balancing plates of homemade chocolate chip cookies and cups of Swiss mocha coffee.

They connected that night, and it was evident that Bonnie really enjoyed Wendi's sharp mind and sense of humor. Wendi opened up about her marriage, her drinking, and her restlessness. Bonnie listened intently but did not offer advice. Instead she told Wendi about her rebellious years and the way she wounded her Christian parents.

"How did you get over it?" asked Wendi.

"I fell in love with Jesus," answered Bonnie.

Wendi's restless sleep was followed by a leisurely breakfast of pancakes and sausage. Then it was back to the quilt room, now on the red cushions. The bumblebees buzzed, and the women engaged in more worship, more Bible teaching. *The Bible—it's an ancient book,* thought Wendi, *but this teacher brings it alive.* Her words pierced Wendi's heart. *She's talking about me again,* thought Wendi.

In the small group, the leader asked questions relating to the message. They grappled with tough issues—like why would God allow Susan's dad to die of cancer, and what was the point of praying if God already knows what's going to happen. Wendi had never participated in a spiritual discussion before. The ideas about God and life fascinated her. Susan recommended a good book.

The afternoon was a smorgasbord. Softball brought back childhood memories of family reunions when Mom and Dad were together, complete with sweat, dirt, and ribbing the losers. After a shower, Bonnie suggested they attend a workshop on how to study the Bible. After years of undergraduate and law school, Wendi knew how to study, but Bible study? How hard could it be? The class wasn't as easy as she thought, but she loved a challenge. And the teacher made it fun.

Saturday night several friends joined Wendi and Bonnie in their room. They rehashed the message and talked about their lives. Wendi listened. After lights out, she lay awake most of the night reflecting. These women loved life. They saw it as an adventure with God—a God who was their Father and guide. And they loved each other. She observed over and over how they included everyone—even the *unlovable* women.

She wondered what they thought about her. Her ideas and life were so different from many of theirs—yet although she was among four hundred strangers, she felt somehow at home. They called themselves Christians, but they weren't the somber, judgmental Christians she'd seen portrayed in the media. Having Bonnie next door comforted Wendi, almost like a family member—the family she'd longed for but never experienced.

Bonnie had invited her to church and Bible study several times. Wendi decided she would go with her next time and see what kind of a church turns out people like this.[6]

Frances's Experience

Dear Lord,

I want to thank you for yourself, for your great love. Thank you for preparing my heart for this last weekend to be with you. I have been your child for fifty-seven years, and I have never been able to really see just how much you loved me. This weekend I finally got to look through the keyhole and see. I believe it started with the Bible study this year as I realized how carefully you put the Garden together for us to be in—we just didn't get to stay there.

You provided Sandra to help me get so comfortable and show me how a retreat worked—you brought the right women to share this dorm. Lord, how special they are! You provided food—those late night snacks were so delicious. As I looked at that table loaded with the fruit you grew, how could I ever thank you enough?

You have given so many gifts to people, and they were willing to use their talents to prepare for this weekend. Our surroundings were carefully planned out—castles, pictures, great entertainment, and gifts!

But Jesus, the most special thing is that you were there. You allowed me to see your love for me as I have never seen it before. What a relief to know how much you love me.

Thanks for Jo Ann coming to help us worship you. Thanks for Jackie, and thank you for being willing to share yourself through her. Thank you for her openness and the experiences of her life. Lord Jesus, I got a glimpse of heaven on Sunday morning and took Communion with you. I just wished you had decided it was time for us all to be in heaven with you on that morning.

As I told Keth all about the retreat, he just smiled and said, "That was a woman's paradise!"

    Thank you for letting me be in paradise with you this weekend. Let me never forget your love and your desire for my love.

I love you, Jesus.

Frances

In this chapter, we've discussed several purposes for a women's retreat. Before you initiate your retreat, know *your* purpose. It is often helpful to write out a purpose statement to keep you and your team focused during the planning stages.

How will you design a retreat that fulfills your purpose and meets the needs of the different women you are serving? Read on.

In Of the Mountain Gods
Ruidoso, N.M.
6 87

Chapter 2

Define Your Parameters

Where, When, and How Long?

Atmosphere influences everything, and every place has its own appeal. Think back to your years as a student. Every teacher created a unique atmosphere in her classroom. Some teachers made asking questions comfortable while others created tension in their space, causing students to fear interacting with them and other students. Every home has an atmosphere too. You may have grown up in a home where you felt unconditionally loved and nurtured, or perhaps you felt you always had to prove yourself. Often without being aware of the significance, we create atmospheres that impact spiritual health and growth—or hinder it.

Where Will You Go?

Where we retreat matters. There are multiple factors to consider, each affecting how women will feel during the retreat experience. And how they feel impacts whether they will be receptive to God's Word, whether they will connect with others, and possibly whether they will make a life-changing decision to enter into a personal relationship with Jesus Christ.

After you specify your purpose, the next decision is to determine where to retreat. The place should complement your purpose. Let's examine some common options.

The Natural Setting or a Luxury Hotel?

"The heavens declare the glory of God; the skies proclaim the work of his hands" (Ps. 19:1). There is something about being in God's creation that causes us to connect with Him and consider eternal questions. The natural setting is the best place to "be still, and know that [he is] God" (Ps. 46:10).

Retreat centers, campgrounds, even farm houses or villas by a lake—they all take us into the country and away from bustling, stressful city life. We recommend holding your retreat in a natural setting if possible—and especially if most of the attendees are city dwellers. Of course, if most of your women live in the country, a retreat in a hotel setting surrounded by interesting shops might offer an exciting change of pace. Again, let your purpose drive your decision.

Wherever you meet, consider these other issues as well.

Where Will You Hold the Main Sessions?

Does the retreat facility have a main room for your entire group to gather to hear the speaker, join in community worship, or hold a talent show? If your group is small this could be the living room of a lake house. If hundreds of women attend, you must be sure you can accommodate the numbers comfortably. Will you need a stage? Sound or audiovisual equipment? Will women be able to see from anywhere in the room?

What kind of atmosphere can you set in the main hall? If you have a large group, can you make it feel intimate? Where will the speaker stand? If she is too distant, she can feel disconnected from the women and they from her. Will they let you decorate? When women remember the retreat, most will probably remember the main sessions first. Be sure you have the facility you need to set the atmosphere and accomplish your purpose.

How Far Will You Have to Travel? How Difficult Is the Location to Find?

Many women don't like to be too far from home. Can you find a location within an hour or two of your church? That's the ideal. However, the ideal isn't always possible. One enterprising group found the perfect location, but it was four hours away. The women were hesitant to drive that far, so they rented buses and included the price of transportation in the retreat price. The bus trip was a highlight of the weekend—a time to meet and bond with new women, to sing together, to unwind, and to enjoy the beautiful scenery.

Even if the site is within an hour or two, connect women so they can carpool together. Provide clear maps and specific directions (for example, turn right at the red barn; left on farm road 32 after the Exxon station). This is especially important if women are driving at night in unfamiliar terrain.

How Comfortable Are the Accommodations?

Liz says her idea of camping is "slow room service." How likely is it that she will sleep on a bunk bed with a two-inch mattress surrounded by fifty other women? On the other hand, Sue's adventurous daughter likes roughing it, especially if it means staying up most of the night talking. Note the variety of women who will be attending your retreat. Can you offer such accommodations that different kinds of women can enjoy the experience? Work toward that ideal, and your retreat will encourage women from different ages and stages, personalities and temperaments, to participate and enrich each other's lives.

What is the ratio of bathroom sinks to participants? Are they clean? On average, Linda has found that one sink to four women allows them minimal waiting time and frustration. In addition, your sessions can start promptly because women made it to breakfast on time.

How's the Food?

Camp food is notoriously lousy! It's difficult to cook for large numbers, but some camps do better than others. Linda "spies out" the facilities and the food before she signs her church up for a retreat there. She sometimes tags along with other churches for a taste-test. If the food is a deterrent, you might make an appointment with the kitchen staff to see if they will work with you on the menu. In addition, you can supplement mediocre meals with snacks provided by the retreat committee. For Sunday morning breakfast, Kelley's retreat team traditionally bought fresh hot cinnamon rolls from a favorite bakery in the town nearby instead of using the retreat center's cafeteria. Extra expenses like these should be included in your budget.

Since hers is a small church, the women usually bring "community" snacks for all to munch on during the weekend. Other options a small group might consider are catering, going out to a local restaurant, or enlisting a team to cook for the group. In some cases, smaller has its advantages over larger.

How Much Can Women Afford?

We would all love to hold our retreat in a luxury villa on the beach or in the mountains, enjoying gourmet meals and afternoons in the spa. However, the cost would keep most women from attending. Brainstorm with women in your church and ask, "What are the priorities of women in our church?" Is food the most important, or is it housing? What will woo them away for a weekend? What would cause women to refuse to participate? Then find a place that best meets the needs of most of your women.

What do churches charge for their retreat? This will vary greatly depending upon your area of the country, the type of facility you choose, the size of your group, and what women are willing to pay. In chapter 5, we will show you how to make a budget, taking into account unexpected expenses and scholarships, so that you will not spend more than you have budgeted.

How Do I Reserve a Site?

Good sites are usually in demand, and you may have to wait to reserve the week you desire. Once you have chosen a site, it's smart to meet with the site host or hostess to foster a relationship. Show them that you will be a valuable customer, considerate of their policies.

Whether you choose a campsite or a hotel, you will probably need to negotiate a contract. This is a legal document that binds you to particular promises. Usually the contract must be signed before the management will reserve the retreat site for you. In the contract you will estimate how many women you expect and will probably have to provide a minimum number. You will agree on the cost of housing, meals, and other services, such as special facilities or activities open to your group. Most contracts clarify the site rules and regulations. Read them carefully and pass them on when needed. See Appendix A for a sample contract.

Dealing with Your Retreat Site Manager

To ensure a successful retreat, foster a cooperative relationship with your retreat site manager or contact person. Establish early on what the manager's preferences are—does he wish to deal with only one member of your team, or is he comfortable dealing with several? Usually your retreat coordinator will act as your main contact with the retreat site manager. After the place and date have been reserved, usually a year or more in advance, the contract is signed and mailed. Be sure you discuss any questions that emerge while reading through the contract—try to eliminate any point of confusion early in the process. It is helpful to sit down face-to-face with the site manager and walk through the contract together.

Circumstances permitting, you may want to bring your lead team to scope out the place a few months in advance as they plan for decorations and theme ideas. Be courteous—call ahead to set up the visit, be attentive and gracious to the site manager as he or she escorts you around. This is your team's chance at a great first impression. You will also want to check in periodically to report the number of expected attendees, communicate any special needs or concerns, and generally keep the communication lines open. As the retreat date draws near, be sure the site manager has given you the name of your weekend contact— the person who will be on call for you should your team need anything during the retreat.

The most important aspect of the relationship between the retreat coordinator and the site manager is good communication. Keep talking, ask questions, be up front about your needs. Be gracious, not demanding. Ask, don't tell. We have found that we accomplish more and establish long-lasting rapport when we phrase our requests, "Can we do this?" rather than, "I need you to perform these tasks for me. . . ."

And don't forget to respect the behavioral and safety guidelines set out for your group by the site manager. Jan-Kay Ranch in Detroit, Texas, doubles as a retreat center and an exotic wildlife refuge. Visitors enjoy the caged tigers and lions, the roaming llamas and camels, and the open petting zoo. But they do not climb the fence into the buffalo pasture for good reason—they could be seriously hurt by a charging bison. Rules are given for the safety and enjoyment of all, so be sure to communicate them to your women.

Will the Site Allow Our Team to Arrive Early to Decorate?

The IBC retreat committee has a tradition of spending the week together on site before the retreat. Of course, not all can attend, but more and more, the women have used this needed time to decorate and set up as an opportunity to bond and cover the retreat in prayer. The team has so much fun, they return to the retreat team year after year. You may not want to arrive that early, but will the site allow you at least a day or two to prepare the atmosphere? Check out the possibilities before you sign on.

When Will You Go?

We live in Texas, and most churches in our region retreat in either the fall or spring—March through May and September through November. Other times are too cold or too hot, especially if you want to enjoy the outdoors. Consider your climate. What works in your region? Remember that summers are often reserved for family vacations. Look at your church calendar to be sure you don't conflict with a major church event.

Choose a time of year when most women can and want to attend. Sue's daughter lives in Anchorage, Alaska, and ChangePoint Church, where she attends, holds four retreats a year, each accommodating no more than one hundred women each time. "Our purpose is to give women opportunity to connect with each other in small groups. We feel we can do this best by keeping the numbers down," says Gwen Adams, director of women's ministries.

The retreat highlight for some Alaskan women is the "polar bear plunge." In the dead of night, women jump into icy cold water as a bonding experience. Afterward, they run into a nearby heated van to towel off and whoop it up! Each receives a certificate "suitable for framing" that authenticates they are members of the polar bear club, making them certified (or is that certifiable?) rugged Alaska women.

How Long Should You Stay?

We recommend spending at least two nights away. We find that women really begin to unwind the second day. If you only stay one night, women never really unplug from life at home. Most retreats occur on weekends—usually beginning Friday night. We have observed that it is often Saturday night and Sunday morning when God works His will. It's important to give Him time.

However, in some churches, the leadership wants you home for worship service, forcing you to return Saturday night or early Sunday morning after a sunrise service. If that's your situation, consider explaining your reasons for staying over on Sunday. Plan your own morning worship service so women feel they aren't missing church. If your leadership still insists on a one-night retreat, make it the best night away you can, and continue to pray that God will soften leadership's hearts. Don't be afraid to reiterate your request each year, in a gracious way, of course. Share stories of changed lives with your leaders. One day they may understand your reasons and grant your request.

You have defined your purpose and established the dates and location. Now it's time to enlist the people—your team and your speaker. Transforming ministry is about people—not programs. Your most important decisions are ahead.

Chapter 3

People Behind the Scenes

Select Your Retreat Team

Choose Your Retreat Coordinator

If your church is blessed with an organized women's ministry led by a women's pastor or director, she will choose the retreat coordinator. In churches without a women's ministry, God sometimes raises up a woman in the congregation with a passion to birth a women's retreat. Often she has attended a retreat, seen the results, and wants this for her own community. If that is you, make an appointment with your senior pastor to ask for permission and support. Share your vision and place yourself under his authority. Ask him to make pulpit announcements and possibly arrange for a budget. Never short-circuit the important step of laying the proper foundation.

Qualities of an Effective Retreat Coordinator

A Passion to Connect Women to God

A successful retreat is fun and entertaining, but that is not its primary purpose. Find a woman who understands that a retreat is about transforming lives through a meaningful experience with God and His community. When the leader focuses on spiritual impact, every decision will reflect this priority.

Administrative Gifts

One of the Greek words for administration, *kubernesis* (1 Cor. 12:28), conjures up the image of a ship's captain. The captain is responsible to get the ship to its final destination. A retreat coordinator is responsible for the planning, execution, and evaluation of the entire retreat. She needs vision to keep the big picture in mind and administrative gifts to delegate the details. Retreats are multifaceted events that require the ability to multitask. A coordinator needs the ability to administer the various tasks skillfully for smooth sailing into "harmony" harbor. Leadership, encouragement, and shepherding gifts are also helpful, especially with larger teams.

People Skills

It takes all kinds of people to implement a retreat that changes lives. The coordinator needs to identify and unleash people with different gift mixes, temperaments, and personalities, placing them in the ministries that best fit them. They need encouragement, development, direction, and, occasionally, exhortation. An effective coordinator shepherds her flock with a balance of finesse and strength. People skills are required.

A Team Builder

A retreat is not a one-woman show. A leader has influence and followers. She builds a team and inspires them to take care of the details. The coordinator must know how to delegate and build a team. Otherwise she will burn out and deprive others of the opportunity to grow and learn. Refer to chapters 4 and 5 of our book *New Doors in Ministry to Women* for valuable insight on building and rallying teams.[1]

Mature and Discerning

Linda slipped into a rehearsal for her retreat's Saturday night talent show to find a line of talented young women moving with precision to the beat of contemporary music. These moms and young career women had choreographed the routine themselves, resurrecting buried talents from high school dance classes and cheerleading routines. It was fun and full of energy, but parts of the routine included some potentially eyebrow-raising moves. Linda called them together, praising their efforts but gently counseling them to "tone down the pelvic thrusts." A truly discerning decision!

A retreat coordinator is responsible for everything that happens at the retreat. She must be willing to make the tough calls, and do it in love.

A Seasonal Commitment

Some women are sprinters, not distance runners. Enlist a sprinter to lead the retreat. Women who travel periodically or have seasonal stresses can't always commit to weekly responsibilities, but they make great event coordinators.

The Retreat Team

What will the retreat team look like? The size of your women's group will determine the size of your team. The smaller the group, the fewer the team members. For example, at Creekside, six women plan a retreat for thirty; IBC uses more than fifteen to plan a retreat for six hundred. In the interest of helping churches of *all* sizes, below we provide a thorough survey of possible team positions. Many of them can be combined with others, some can be bypassed completely, and others can wait until the specific need arises. It all depends on your size. If you are a small-church leader, pick and choose which positions are most necessary to your situation. Some positions we list are responsible for tasks that a small church may not include—T-shirts and special gifts, for instance. With your own church's needs in mind, take a look at a variety of retreat team positions.

Program Coordinator

The program coordinator is responsible for setting the atmosphere of the retreat, specifically the main sessions. She works with the retreat coordinator to plan the sessions, focusing primarily on the "interrupts." These are five- to ten-minute light, often humorous, dramas that introduce each session and complement the retreat theme. The interrupts are an icebreaker, tearing down walls of nervousness and fear, disarming newcomers and unbelievers. Often the actors joust verbally with the emcee in playful satire or comedy. Proverbs 17:22 says, "A cheerful heart is good medicine, but a crushed spirit dries up the bones." Laughter unites the women in community and helps them relax.

The program director oversees the scriptwriting, set design, music, choice of cast, rehearsals, and costumes for each interrupt. In the second half of this book, we will provide numerous examples of interrupts for you to use as you learn to create your own. You may want to create simple interrupts or more elaborate ones, depending on your budget and resources.

After-hour games and free-time options such as baseball and volleyball tournaments, horseback riding, and canoeing may also fall under the responsibilities of the program coordinator. Interactive games that relate to your theme build friendships and give women opportunity to take off their "responsibility" hats and act silly for a time. Again, we will provide examples in the latter section of this book.

Find a creative, artistic woman for this role and unleash her. You'll be amazed at the ideas she and her team generate. She also needs people skills to motivate her team and the discipline to work ahead. Her work is important in setting the mood of the retreat, making women comfortable and more open to God's work in their lives.

Registration Coordinator

The registration coordinator is the first contact most women will have with the retreat, so she should be a gracious woman. Her role is critical to a successful experience. She handles the sign-ups, collects money, and makes room assignments. If there are limited accommodations, she negotiates with late-comers who are displeased with their rooms or roommates. Find a woman with administrative abilities and computer skills. If your retreat is large, she may want to create a database to help her with great quantities of information. She sends out a confirmation letter, a map, a list of items to bring, and any other information needed to help women find the retreat center, navigate their way around it, and locate their room.

She may oversee transportation and carpooling, and she may help the retreat coordinator choose the facility. Some registration coordinators make name tags and help women check in. Usually she is on duty all of Friday night, and she's the last one to leave on Sunday, checking the rooms at the end for lost items. It's important that she be cordial and fair, never giving special favors to her friends. If the retreat appears unorganized, women will not invest their time in attending. This position is key to the overall excellence a successful retreat requires.

Worship Leader

The main sessions usually begin with a light, humorous mood and shift into a more serious tone as the women prepare to hear the speaker. A skilled, inspired worship leader is key to preparing the hearts of the women to hear what God wants to say to them during the retreat. Usually worship leaders come from within your church family, but if you bring in a guest, recruit a worship coordinator from your church to be her liaison and hostess. The second half of chapter 4 focuses on the worship leader's qualifications and calling.

Prayer Coordinator

A retreat that changes lives is founded on prayer, both before and during the weekend. A prayer coordinator facilitates prayer for the leaders, speakers, and participants. Once registration begins, she sends out lists of the names to her team, who commit to cover the retreat with prayer. Consider creative ways to make each woman feel special: take a prayer walk around the retreat site asking the Lord to bless every moment of the event, pray for each woman name by name and face by face, and sit in each chair and pray for the women who will be occupying it. Remember, however you choose to pray, just do it!

Decorations Coordinator

The decor sets the scene throughout the facility and during the main sessions. These theme props can be as simple or elaborate as resources allow. Look for a woman who loves power tools or is a whiz with a sewing machine. This is the team member who brings the theme alive. Encourage her to recruit a team of handywomen who love to create, paint, sew, and saw. Then let them go and stand back.

One thrifty and creative decorations coordinator was constantly looking for ways to illustrate their group's western theme. While out driving, she spied a trailer full of old fence posts. She flagged down the driver and asked if he would donate them to the retreat. He delivered them to her friend's back yard, where they were stored, awaiting the anticipated weekend.

In our final chapters, we will give you a variety of examples and patterns to help prime your own creative pump as you illustrate your retreat through decorations.

Hospitality Coordinator

When women celebrate, they want food! Your hospitality coordinator's ministry may simply be to ask the women to bring their favorite snacks and arrange them in an attractive display, or she may prepare large amounts of food herself for either a meal or intermittent snacking. If so, she needs a background in food preparation, understanding how much food per person, and related information. She may be gifted at soliciting donations. This is often a thankless job, so look for a woman with the gift of serving who enjoys staying behind the scenes.

Notebook Coordinator

Provide a notebook with all the information needed for the weekend. This is a great way to promote other ministries your church might offer, without taking time for verbal announcements. The retreat is often an entry point into the church, so be sure to show women how they can get involved in Bible study or other important women's ministry functions.

A retreat notebook includes the weekend schedule; biographies of the speaker and the worship leader; descriptions of breakout sessions; words to songs; Bible passages requested by the speaker; a place to take notes during the lectures; small group discussion questions; opportunities to plug into other ministries; maps; and letters from the retreat coordinator, women's pastor, or senior pastor. IBC takes pictures of all the participants, and women use this pictorial guide not only at the retreat but also throughout the year to connect to women and link names and faces.

The notebook coordinator needs computer skills as well as administrative gifts. If she includes pictures, she will need to recruit a photographer or act as one herself.

Small-Groups Coordinator

Connecting with new friends is a retreat highlight, and relationships are often birthed in small groups.

The small-groups coordinator recruits leaders and assigns women to groups. She may train the leaders if needed and work with the speaker to create good discussion questions that complement her messages.

The small-groups coordinator needs to know women in the church so she can find skilled leaders who will create a warm, accepting atmosphere. A leader needs a shepherd's heart and Bible knowledge so she can minister to hurting women assigned to her group. We will explain ways to group your women and other tips to make small groups work in chapter 5.

Entertainment Coordinator

If you include a talent show in your format, you will need a coordinator to oversee its production. Give women a platform to express their creativity. You'll be surprised how many studied drama in college or love to sing but have few outlets for their talents. IBC women formed a tap dance company that performs yearly. Working women, moms, and grandmothers practice long hours and delight in resurrecting this talent.

Find a woman who loves to encourage others to use their creative gifts and give her the resources to produce a show that is fun and not too competitive. You'll be amazed at what you see, and this portion of the retreat will become a tradition that draws women year after year.

Breakout Workshops Coordinator

Your church is full of women with gifts and talents they seldom have the opportunity to share. Breakout workshops on a variety of topics—from prayer to pastries, running to relationships—connect women in smaller sessions and give them a chance to learn a new skill or gain needed information. These sessions are always optional on a Saturday afternoon for women who don't want to nap, go into town antiquing, or play volleyball.

Design these workshops with the felt needs of the participants in mind. Be sure to include one on parenting if many of the participants are moms with young children, or one on aging parents if your ranks are full of empty nesters. Be sure to include lighthearted topics such as crafts or cooking in addition to heavier, more substantial themes like intimacy or spiritual growth. An added benefit to breakout workshops is that leaders often discover women with teaching gifts whom they can plug into other ministries later.

Your coordinator needs to scout quality speakers, plan ahead, and possess good communication skills. She will need to oversee the logistics of each workshop, advertise it well, and provide for the audiovisual needs of the speakers. Breakout sessions are optional, but they add variety and are a draw as your retreat grows larger.

Serendipity Team Member

"Serendipity" means an unexpected surprise. As your budget allows, lavish special surprises on the participants throughout the retreat to make them know how much they are loved. These can range from chocolate candy on their pillow to a lovely plaque under their chair or a piece of simple jewelry reminding them of the theme or speaker's application. If these kinds of gifts are too expensive, put your "crafty" women to work during the year making something that reminds the women of God's message for them during the weekend. Find a woman with the gift of giving and ask her to subsidize the gifts. If you plan ahead, you can make every woman feel God's love, regardless of your resources.

Speaker Hostess

Speaking at a retreat is hard work. Your teacher has probably spent a minimum of twenty hours to write each message. Then she must internalize each one in turn, requiring a block of time at home before she arrives and time between each message to refresh. In addition, a good retreat speaker will want to spend time with women between sessions who have questions or need encouragement. You can be sure your speaker goes home exhausted. How can you encourage her, making the experience as memorable and pleasant as possible?

Provide someone to ensure that her accommodations are conducive to study and preparation as well as a good night's sleep. The speaker hostess can sit with the speaker at meals and introduce her to women in the church, especially if she is a guest. Providing water by the podium and meals in her room if she needs time to prepare are simple ways to show the love of Christ and undergird the speaker, making her more effective as she speaks God's Word to the women. Let her know women are praying for her.

Choose a hostess with gifts of hospitality and encouragement, maybe someone she already knows. Then challenge her to do everything she can to make the speaker feel included and special. The dividends will be evident in the lives of the women she ministers to all weekend and beyond.

Chapter 4

Up-Front People

*U*ntil you have established a retreat tradition at your church, your speaker is often what draws women to attend. She proclaims the Word of God. She is the model of what Jesus can do in women's lives. In a sense, she is the Lord's representative, speaking on His behalf to woo women into a personal relationship with Jesus Christ and to build up those who already know Him.

Choose Your Speaker

The speaker sets the spiritual tone of the retreat, making it an inspiring, God-glorifying experience—or a letdown. Choose your speaker carefully and prayerfully.

Questions to Consider

Is She Grounded in God's Word?

To transform lives, choose a Bible teacher. Be sure she teaches messages based on the Scriptures and sound doctrine. You may want her to affirm your church's doctrinal statement to ensure her beliefs are similar to those of your church. Often friends or women in your church will recommend speakers they hear. Keep a record of these names to draw from when you are ready to begin the selection process.

There are many ways to evaluate whether a speaker is a good match for your retreat. Explore her church background and training. Ask for references and check them out. Find out where she has spoken before and ask other retreat coordinators for their feedback. Listen to taped messages or, even better, attend a retreat or luncheon to observe not only the content of her message but also her demeanor and body language. Watch how she interacts with her hostess and the women attending. Discern whether her message is based on the Bible or if she simply interjects a Bible verse occasionally to give it a spiritual flavor.

Is Her Bible Message Interesting, Relevant, and Applicable?

It's wrong for speakers to bore people with the Bible, but they still do. If your speaker is dry, unable to connect or relate to women's everyday needs, she can ruin the retreat. Find a speaker who is passionate about ministering to women, one who knows issues women today face, and who will challenge them with measurable goals to apply after they leave.

Is She a Skilled, Gifted Communicator?

God gifts some women with the ability to teach, and some of these women develop that gift. Find a woman who loves to teach God's Word and is good at it. You can tell by listening. A gifted teacher connects with her audience. She presents her material in ways that are easily grasped by the newcomer and the veteran. Her content is valuable, something to ponder and chew on. She loves to study and pass on what God teaches her. She is interesting, often humorous, but her message is more than entertaining. It has solid, meaty substance that changes lives, and it is delivered with winsome words and clarity.

Is She Mature?

Once a gifted young woman in her early twenties asked her older Bible teacher if she could join the teaching team. The older teacher answered, "But, my dear, what would you have to say?" Certainly the teacher did not mean that this young woman had nothing to offer. However, she had not lived long enough to have very much to say about life. Find a woman who has walked with the Lord long enough to have something meaningful to say. This does not necessarily correspond to chronological age, but often age is a factor. Kelley's church enjoys hearing from experienced women and generally selects women over forty to speak at their retreats. On the other hand, if your audience is all early twenties, a sixty-year-old may not be able to relate to them.

Is She Real?

Speakers who give the impression they are perfection personified are liars. Although your speaker should be an example of the difference Christ can make, she also erects walls rather than bridges by refusing to admit her own limitations and shortcomings. Find a speaker who is a fellow struggler, yet an overcomer. Ask her to tell her story early in the retreat, especially if she is a stranger. As she opens up her life to the women who attend, they will open up their lives to one another. Then the process of healing can begin.

Is She Personable?

Sue experienced an unfortunate choice in speakers. Once we flew in a famous speaker who charged a sizable fee and marketed her books after every message. As she finished her talk, she darted off behind the curtain where Sue was standing. In a huff, she ordered Sue to get her purse. Sheepishly, Sue retrieved her purse, which the speaker snatched out of her hand and then ran out as if the church were on fire. Sue remembers thinking, "What a waste of the Lord's money." No matter how good the speaker, if she doesn't spend time with the women, she sabotages her message.

Of course, if she speaks three or four times, she may need time alone to prepare. But once her preparation is complete, you want a speaker who connects with women one-on-one or in groups, especially with women who have questions or need a special word of counsel. Speakers who join women at meals, sit to talk and pray after main sessions, and take time to greet women beforehand show the heart of Jesus and back up their words with action.

What is her heart attitude? Is she a superstar, an entertainer there to make a name for herself—or does she genuinely care about the women she is teaching? For a retreat that changes lives, choose a speaker who cares rather than a prima donna.

We have described the perfect speaker, but she doesn't actually exist. Many Bible teachers are trained on the retreat circuit, and they won't always measure up to the standards we just set. But many desire to honor God and minister to women wholeheartedly. Look for a speaker like that—with a heart attitude to serve and a willingness to learn. Discern which qualities are most important for your women that year. Ask God to enable you to find His choice, and He will guide you to just the speaker that can join your team and make the retreat one your women won't forget.

Should She Be "Homegrown" or a Guest?

During IBC's twenty-four year retreat history, they have alternated each year between a homegrown speaker and a guest speaker. What are the advantages of using speakers from your church? The women know her, and she can continue her ministry to them when they all return home. In addition, she knows the needs of the women and works well with the retreat team—she already knows them. There are women with the gift of teaching in your midst. Identify them and give them an opportunity to minister. When you do, you groom them for other kinds of ministry and show women that God can use us all.

It is also fun to hear from a guest, but you will need to research her more carefully. It's exciting to hear from someone new, especially if she is respected, known around your town—but you also run the risk of a surprise. If you do your homework, though, you can find a guest speaker who is just right for your retreat.

Is This the Right Time?

If your potential speaker alerts you to a crisis situation in her life, you may want to wait and ask her another time. A retreat coordinator's nightmare is a phone call the week before informing her the speaker can't come—and that does happen. If she or a family member is facing a health crisis or another possible obstacle, God may be giving you a red flag. If her church is in the midst of a church split, wait for it to settle. If you don't, her situation will distract from her ministry and possibly foster gossip, as curious women want to know what's going on.

How Do You Recruit a Speaker?

Pray about the names of recommended women, asking God to reveal His choice for that year's retreat. He alone knows the needs of the women who will be attending. Remember to work with one speaker at a time. If you ask several to speak at your retreat, they all may say yes. If you cannot work out the details with one, then you know she isn't God's choice, and you begin the process again with another.

As you pray about God's choice, you may want to ask prior retreat team members or other ministry leaders to give you feedback on your options. If you need to listen to taped messages, call the speaker and ask if she can provide them, or try to locate tapes from another source. It is premature at this time to tell her she is a candidate for your retreat. If you like the taped message, it is ideal to see her in person speaking at another event.

Once you believe this speaker may be God's choice, contact her by phone to learn about her availability and fee. If these meet with your approval, explain your expectations. How many messages would she deliver? Are there other meetings you want her to attend? If she is positive about the possibility, ask her to pray and tell her you will call her back, giving her a time frame when she can expect to hear from you.

If she accepts the invitation, meet face to face. Now is the time to work out details. If she isn't local, set up a time for an extended phone call. There are important details you need to agree on.

What Do the Women Need to Hear?

Often a retreat speaker will have three or four prepared retreat packages to choose from—subjects that are her passion. You know the women who will be attending. Does one of these subjects meet their particular needs right now? If not, is the speaker willing to create new retreat messages for you? Preparation time may be up to eighty hours for four new messages. Some speakers simply do not have the time. Others are willing. Take this into account when you pay her. If you cannot agree, she may not be the speaker for you this year. Once you have agreed on the subject, you can begin brainstorming the theme. Your retreat theme will probably complement the Bible messages.

What Will You Pay Her?

Fees vary from speaker to speaker. Professional speakers and authors often have a set fee, sometimes thousands of dollars. Some charge a percentage of your intake and require a certain number of participants. Authors want to sell their books, and some even bring a team to oversee their sales. If she is traveling, you are expected to pay airfare or mileage as well as accommodations and meals. Most churches can't afford a professional speaker and instead look for a woman in their locale. There are probably a number of excellent speakers right in your back yard. Talk to women at other churches to solicit their opinions.

Most local speakers do not charge a set fee but work with the church on the amount. What is reasonable? Find out what a speaker normally is paid in your area for a luncheon and multiply by the number of messages. Explain to the speaker if you have a limited budget, and she may be willing to speak for less. Work out these details up front.

Where Can You Find Speakers?

Your location and size will determine the resources available to you. In the "Bible Belt" of the South, it is difficult *not* to find any number of qualified speakers—seminaries, Bible colleges, large churches, and parachurch ministries abound. But many churches are not nestled in the heart of evangelicalism as we are, and retreat teams are greatly challenged to find and book a speaker who will meet their needs.

Ministry is about people—not programs. And your speaker is key to your retreat's success. Linda calls the speaker search a lifestyle. She is always on the alert for an effective communicator. After you have identified God's choice for your speaker, you are ready to make another important decision: who will lead the worship?

Choose Your Worship Leader

What is worship? Worship leader Mary Bodien describes worship as "responding to God." A retreat is a time to praise God for who He is and what He is doing in our lives. Worship should not be an afterthought. It sets the atmosphere and prepares women's hearts to hear God's Word. It builds community and engages women as they participate together to tell God through music how much they love and adore Him.

As you recruit your worship leader, look for a woman who does not view her role as performer or entertainer. Instead, find someone who delights in leading women to God's throne where they unite hearts and voices in corporate praise.

Before you recruit her, decide on her role and communicate clearly. Be sure she knows what you expect. Will she also serve as the master of ceremonies? Will you pay her? What kind of music are you expecting? Who will accompany her, and what resources are available at the retreat facility? Will she be expected to meet with the speaker to coordinate the music and the messages?

What Makes an Excellent Retreat Worship Leader?

- *The worship leader should know the audience.* Acquaint her with the kinds of women attending. What is the age range? Do the women enjoy traditional hymns, praise music, or both? Only if she knows who is coming will she choose music that works.
- *The worship leader should choose songs the women know.* Meeting with the retreat leaders and the speaker enables the worship leader to choose music that is familiar. Mary Bodien has a list of about fifty songs to choose from. She may introduce a new song that complements the passages or theme, but the general menu is recognizable.
- *The worship leader should know how many sessions you expect and the length of each.* We suggest that you include music during each session. Our churches

plan for at least twenty minutes before the speaker begins. Allot enough time for the women to wind down from previous activities and focus their minds on the Lord. This segment may include corporate singing, special music by an ensemble or a soloist, related responsive readings, an instrumental, a poetry reading, or any other creative addition that focuses on worship. Mary suggests no more than one special song per session.

- *The worship leader should connect with the speaker before the retreat.* The two meet to discuss topics, pertinent Scripture passages, and suggested songs. If the speaker has manuscripts of her messages, it is helpful to share them with the worship leader. When the speaker and worship leader communicate the flow of ideas session by session, the words and music can be woven together to form a powerful message that changes lives.

- *The worship leader should enlist a team.* The word "TEAM" is an acrostic for "Together Everyone Accomplishes More." A worship leader leads not only the worship during the retreat but also a team of women who offer their vocal and instrumental gifts and talents to the Lord. The worship leader needs to coordinate this team and meet with them to rehearse before they arrive. They should work ahead as much as possible.

  The team will include a minimum of one lead instrument, usually a piano or guitar. Don't use recorded accompaniment for the majority of your music, with the exception of special music. Be sure you rehearse with the instruments you will be using if possible.

  It is effective to enlist an ensemble of three to five women to join the worship leader on stage. The sound is fuller, and the group brings energy to the worship time. Your ensemble can be composed of different volunteers each session or a more polished trio or quartet. If you use volunteers, women have the opportunity to try something new, and you have the chance to identify women for the future. If you use a more polished group, the quality is generally better. The choice is yours. The worship leader may want to identify one person to lead the worship groups and coordinate the rehearsals.

Should Your Worship Leader Be "Homegrown" or Recruited from the Outside?

If you find a woman from within your church who loves worship and is a gifted musician and communicator, use her. But if no one surfaces, don't be afraid to find a "professional" and pay her to lead worship and train women in your own congregation. Except for your speaker, no one can do more to help or hinder the retreat than your worship leader. Choose her carefully and prayerfully.

Chapter 5

Prepare Ahead

You have nailed down preliminary decisions—defined your purpose, secured your date and place, and determined your up-front and behind-the-scenes people. But you have not finished planning. There are still important decisions to consider before you actually begin to construct the retreat. At the risk of repeating ourselves, we want to stress that these decisions will be influenced by the size of your group. Small churches may likely reach the goals of intimacy, fun, and solid teaching and worship with less money and time than will the larger churches. The issues we address in this chapter are once again adaptable to the individual group, so filter our suggestions through the grid of your reality, your situation.

The Theme

The theme is the hook that draws women, enticing them to set aside several days out of their busy lives. Take time to create a theme that will attract non-believers as well as women in the church. Enlist wordsmiths to help you. Make it fun, possibly with a double meaning or underlying spiritual message. For example, one year, IBC marketed their retreat as a cruise on the *S. S. Tarara*. Their brochure looked like a slick travel brochure from an elite cruise line, touting the finest in maritime traveling. Women who dreamed of one day taking a cruise pretended they could finally afford it as excitement built before the anticipated weekend.

When the women arrived, they learned that *Tarara* is Ararat spelled backward, and they were actually "sailing" on Noah's ark, together with life-size animal couples peppering the camp and a twenty-foot replica of the ark on the front lawn. (Instructions for the ship and animals will be included in our final "how to" section.) The retreat speaker sculpted her messages around Genesis 6–9, tying the spiritual content to the overall retreat theme. This may not always be possible, but if you can pull it off, expect maximum impact.

Sometimes the spiritual theme comes first. For example, another year the retreat leader recruited a speaker and a retreat package she had used previously, titled "The Cross, the Crook, and the Crown" from Psalms 22–24. The retreat team played off the spiritual messages that included the Shepherd and sheep with a nursery rhyme theme. Mother Goose, Mary with her little lamb, Little Bo Peep, and Little Boy Blue showed up in full costume, marching down the aisle to a jazzed up version of "Baa, Baa, Black Sheep" to send the women into stitches every session. This theme carried through to the entertainment, the giveaways, and decorations.

Choose a theme that is fun or intriguing, then unleash your artists, designers, musicians, and craftswomen to illustrate the concepts. You may have to search for these artists at first. In many churches, there are few opportunities for artists to serve, but once you discover them, they will be a treasure that you can draw on often. And they will delight in the chance to minister this way.

On Sunday we usually change the main stage scenery to reflect a more reverent and worshipful atmosphere. We don't use the lighter, humorous interrupts but instead try to create a time when women reflect on what they have learned during the weekend about their relationship with God. For a detailed example, see chapter 11, "Candlelight Backdrop."

Art

The Great Commission instructs Christians to "make disciples" of all people regardless of age, race, or place (Matt. 28:19–20). Art speaks across barriers and is especially effective with postmoderns. In our first book, *New Doors in Ministry to Women,* we defined the postmodern woman as "twenty-something" and the modern woman as over thirty years old.[1] If we do not intentionally design our retreats for women of all ages and stages and from all places, we dishonor God and His mandate in the Great Commission. And it's more fun when a variety of women participate.

"Because individual women learn, worship, and experience things differently, we will reach more women by using more than one methodology. And variety keeps things interesting!" says Julie Pierce, IBC's associate pastor to women. For insight into how to include both the modern and postmodern in your planning, we recommend chapters 1 and 9 of *New Doors in Ministry to Women.*[2]

When we use art to illustrate our theme and spiritual message, we make the retreat an experience for all.

What is art? Edith Schaeffer says,

> Whatever it is, surely art involves *creativity* and *originality*. Whatever form art takes, it gives outward expression to what otherwise would remain locked in the mind, unshared. One individual personality has definite or special talent for expressing in *some* medium, what other personalities can hear, see, smell, feel, taste, understand, enjoy, be stimulated by, be involved in, find refreshment in, find satisfaction in, find fulfillment in, experience reality in, be agonized by, be pleased by, enter into, but which they could *not* produce themselves.
>
> Art in various forms expresses and gives opportunity to others to share in, and respond to, things which would otherwise remain vague, empty yearnings. Art satisfies and fulfills something in the people creating and in those responding.[3]

How can you use art in your retreat? Give women a saw and a paintbrush and ask them to design the decor. Ask a woman to sign the words to the worship music. Use film clips, ceremony, pictures, paintings, drama, poetry, and dance to bring the theme and spiritual messages alive. Art drives them deep into women's souls. Ask women what they remember a year later. Often it is the art that implanted the message within. Ellen Theilen, a member of the arts integration team at IBC, observes, "No matter how many walls we build around us, they can always be penetrated through our senses and emotions, and often art can make those walls crumble."

Using art is sometimes challenging at a retreat center. You may have to haul everything back and forth, and the center may not have the technology you are used to in your church (or there may be more). Know your facility and communicate the resources to your speaker, worship leader, and team. Improvise. The hard work to make it happen will pay off in eternal dividends.

Budget

If only money were not an issue in ministry. But since that will never happen, you'll need a plan to manage your budget for the retreat. As with any financial issue, your main questions to answer are what are the expenses, and how will they be paid?

Based on your budget, or lack thereof, you must first determine a price to charge each attendee. We'll walk you through the decision-making process at both a small and a large church to help bring this to life.

Creekside's women typically retreat in the fall at an encampment almost two hours out of the Dallas area. The retreat center provided a set price per person of $40, which included lodging, three meals on Saturday, and a campfire time on Saturday night in their outdoor amphitheater. We chose to forego the Sunday breakfast, which would have added another $5 per person, in favor of bringing in hot rolls from a local bakery (less cost, better taste). The center required that we pay for a minimum of twenty-five women, a number we sometimes were able to exceed or meet—sometimes not. Twenty-five people times $40 equals $1,000.

Then we added our $300 speaker fee, plus the hot rolls and any other special expense. Let's add $100 to round it out. The total, $1,400, is then divided into 25, making $56 per person. That figure is the absolute lowest we could go to break even, so we tacked on another $4 per person to make it an even $60. The extra $4 helped cover part of the decorations and equipment costs too. But many of those items were donated by women serving on the retreat team.

What about donations? In small churches, many of the creative touches, decorations, and gifts cannot be included in a tiny budget. Regardless of size, having a woman on your team who can seek out donations from companies and individuals can reap a creative windfall. From mints to cards to even larger gifts, you never know what you might be given freely if you don't ask around. The motto of the retreat team at Grace Chapel in Lexington, Massachusetts, is "Beg, borrow, but do not steal." And never be afraid to let your congregation know that their special, one-time financial gift toward the women's retreat is not only appreciated but needed. Communicate with your church leadership as well—perhaps there is money in the overall budget they might send your way.

How do the finances work in a large church? The basic principles are the same: determine a price per person based on available funds and donations, the cost set by the retreat center, and costs incurred by the retreat team for decorations. You may also want to consider costs for items such as supplies for more elaborate decorations, printed brochures and other publicity, notebooks, T-shirts and tote bags, golf carts, food, costumes, and special gifts. But remember that more isn't necessarily better—be purposeful in your decisions, being good stewards of the money God has entrusted to you.

About Scholarships

In every church, some women find themselves unable to afford the cost of a retreat. In an ideal world, no woman would be left at home due to insufficient funds—scholarships would be available for every need. But extra money isn't limitless, so how should a retreat coordinator divide the scholarship fund? What principles should guide her decisions?

For simplicity's sake, we suggest you have a form available for women to complete, stating their basic contact information as well as a brief description of their financial circumstances. You may include such questions as:

- Why do you need financial help? (This helps define a true need.)

- Have you received a scholarship for a past retreat? (Is this a pattern for anyone?)

- How much can you give toward the cost? (Many times women can contribute a small amount if they plan ahead and sacrifice a few small things over time. Encourage a sense of ownership.)

- What ministries are you involved in at church? (You may give preference to women who contribute to the body.)

(See appendix C for a sample scholarship form.)

Don't publicize the fact that you offer scholarships. People who need them will ask. In small churches, you may know the women needing help and offer a scholarship to them. The coordinator should make these decisions and maintain confidentiality. After your retreat coordinator has determined her budget for scholarships and who should receive them, she should send a letter to each recipient welcoming her to the retreat and informing her of the amount granted. Often, staff women and pastors' wives are given scholarships as a thank-you for their service to the church. Create a policy to guide your decisions—this will help avert any accusations of favoritism or bias in the awarding of scholarships. Don't be afraid to let the church know of the ministry's need for scholarship money. If possible, make (or have the pastor make on your behalf) an appeal from the pulpit. Such giving blesses not only the recipients but also the givers.

Worship

Song Selection

The time of worship through singing at a retreat is critical because it enables women to focus on God and to express to Him their love and appreciation for who He is and what He has done. Corporate worship through singing is an opportunity to respond to God through music. Numerous psalms speak directly about singing to the Lord.

There is also an aspect of teaching involved in corporate singing. Carefully chosen music can fulfill the directive in Colossians 3:16 to "teach and admonish one another with all wisdom, and as you sing psalms, hymns and spiritual songs with gratitude in your hearts to God." Unfortunately, many songs today teach false or weak doctrine, so it is imperative that the worship leader carefully scrutinize lyrics when choosing the music to be sung at a retreat. Sometimes "our favorites" are not the best choices.

It is critical that the worship leader and retreat speaker partner together. They should set up a meeting or phone conference as far in advance of the retreat as possible. The worship leader is seeking not only a synopsis of each message but, even more so, the speaker's vision for the retreat. That enables the worship leader both to prepare music that correlates with the messages and to pray in accordance with what God has put on her heart.

Some speakers want the worship leader to select all the music; others are willing to give input. If a song or list of songs is suggested, it is important to consider whether they are songs that are familiar to the women and would work well with the instrumentation and style that is being planned for the retreat.

Important considerations regarding song selection:

> Worship is when you're aware that what you've been given is far greater than what you can give. Worship is the awareness that were it not for His touch, you'd still be hobbling and hurting, bitter and broken. Worship is the "thank you" that refuses to be silenced![4]
>
> —Max Lucado

> Worship is the total adoring response of man to one Eternal God, self-revealed in time.[5]
>
> —Evelyn Underhill

1. Pray, pray, pray!
2. Read key Bible passages related to each lesson.
3. Consider any song requests from the speaker. Note: It is ultimately the worship leader's responsibility to make wise music selections, so do not let the speaker's song requests drive the choice of music. Weigh the requests carefully. Use them if possible, but do not be ruled by them.
4. Make a list of possible songs.
5. Choose songs from that list, considering keys, tempo, style, instrumentation, transitions, and familiarity.
   - For example, if you are using only a piano, then carefully consider whether a song is guitar- or percussion-driven and whether it can be done effectively with piano only.
   - Consider beginning with songs of adoration and praise, then moving to one or two reflective or teaching songs at the end of the worship set.
   - Include Scripture readings and prayer in the worship set.
   - The majority of the songs used should be familiar to most of the women who will attend the retreat. It is very difficult for women to worship if they are having to learn a new song at the same time. However, don't be afraid to introduce one or two new songs at a retreat that can be repeated throughout the weekend. This creates a special sort of "retreat ethos" when all attending have learned the same song together.
6. Know how much time has been allotted for worship and honor that. After songs are selected, time them and adjust the set as needed.
7. Rehearse, rehearse, rehearse! The worship of the congregation will be as effective as the worship of its leader. If the leader is struggling through music that is ill prepared, the women will be distracted and ill at ease, which inhibits worship.
8. Worship, worship, worship! "My goal is always to truly worship as I am leading," says Mary Bodien. "That is possible only when I am well prepared both spiritually and musically. That takes time and intention! When I am leading, I have a sort of 'blend into the woodwork' philosophy. My heart's desire is to get out of the way so that God can lead."

Worship Team

What about a worship team? If there are singers or instrumentalists in your church who love to worship, use them. Building a gifted and well-prepared team increases the depth of the musical and spiritual capacity of worship. Look for women who have:

1. A heart for worship—this is not a performance, and there are no "stars." God is the focus, not the musicians. Note: We suggest the worship leader meet one-on-one with musicians she does not know before placing them on a worship team. This gives her an opportunity to become familiar with their spiritual walk and their musical experience and ability. It also allows them the opportunity to get to know her priorities and style as a worship leader.
2. Musical talent:
    *   Consider voice parts—a worship team of four altos doesn't work very well.
    *   Consider vocal quality and ability to blend with others.
    *   For instrumentalists, will her instrument and ability be an enhancement to this team, considering style and level of difficulty? Remember that as instruments are added, more rehearsal time is normally required.
3. Willingness to attend rehearsals and learn new music.

Transitions

When selecting music for a worship set, consider carefully the transition from song to song. Choosing songs that are in compatible keys and stylistically lend themselves to a flow that leads to true worship is the first step, but you must also decide exactly how you plan to get from one song to the next. Will you say anything or just move right into the next song without speaking? Will you simply stop one song and start another, or will an instrument play a musical transition to lead you into the next piece?

If you are not comfortable with making musical transitions on the piano or other instrument, learn some basic transition chords or modulations, and practice them until you are very comfortable playing them. Also, choose carefully what you as the worship leader will or will not say between songs. A good rule of thumb is the old saying "Less is more." A few carefully chosen words, especially Scripture, can be a powerful part of worship and lead the worshiper with ease from song to song. But beware of distracting your women with too many words, and remember that your job is not to be the preacher. Allow an opportunity for women to commune with God without constant interruption. And, finally, rehearse the transitions as you are practicing the worship set. Transitioning is a critical part of the set that is often overlooked. Remember that your goal is to arrange a set of worship songs that flow smoothly from one to the next so that the worshipers can focus fully on God.

Small Groups

Modern and postmodern women love fellowship. God created women relational, as a reflection of His triune character. Women should never be ashamed of enjoying relationships. Building relationships—first with Jesus and then with each other—is second only to centering on Scripture. Small groups are the means to relationship and thus transformation.

Therefore, you are wise to invest prayer, time, and resources into building your small groups. It is a key priority. The best small groups are mixed in age, spiritual maturity, and life-stage experiences. Because of the biblical mandate in Titus 2, God desires that we put women of different ages together. If we teach the younger women to take the initiative, natural Titus 2 mentoring friendships emerge out of the mixed small group. In addition, it is healthy for women to come in contact with all kinds of women.

There are a variety of ways to divide your women into small groups during a retreat. It all depends on how many women are attending. With a small church, the retreat coordinator has the benefit of knowing almost every woman personally and can place each one according to her needs, personality, and ability to contribute. She'll know which leaders can handle a talkative woman or one with heavy issues to tackle or where to place unbelievers and visitors. Small numbers make this job fairly simple.

Dividing larger groups can be more challenging. The easiest method gathers women together based on their room assignments. This gives them more opportunity for getting to know their cabin mates, and it is optimal for six- to ten-member small groups, the best size to encourage intimacy without intimidation. If your rooming arrangement doesn't lend itself well to small group formation, perhaps you could divide your women by which church service they attend. That way they get to know women they will see weekly at church.

While the goal in dividing up your women is to mix up the generations—putting grandmothers and young mothers together, for instance— there are some occasions when that won't be possible or preferable. Sometimes it is beneficial to include special interest groups such as college age, singles, mothers of toddlers, and the like. This, of course, puts women of similar ages and circumstances together. Take the pulse of your women to see which special groups would be appreciated. There are any number of ways to create small groups— you'll have to be creative each year.

Chapter 6

Process

Make It Happen!

*N*ow it's time for fun—constructing the retreat. You are prayed up, your people are in place, and you've made key decisions that fit your women and your purpose. In this chapter we provide a calendar to tweak depending on your size and setting. The larger your group and the more complex the retreat, the longer the range of planning required.

Six Months Out

Meet with the Speaker

The coordinator should initiate time with the speaker to form a friendship and to clarify expectations. The coordinator knows the audience and can help the speaker design Bible messages to meet those particular needs. What is the spiritual background of the women coming? Are they primarily from your church? Do you expect nonbelievers to attend? Are there women from a variety of theological perspectives that the speaker needs to consider?

The speaker needs to know how many times you want her to speak and how long you want her to speak at each session. Do you prefer that she begin with a testimony so the women can get to know her personally? If so, this is the time to tell her.

The speaker also needs a timeline of requests from the coordinator. For example, is the coordinator expecting the speaker to write the small group discussion questions? If so, the speaker needs some guidelines. How many small group sessions are planned? How many questions will be needed at each session? Give special instructions like "Keep the first session's questions nonthreatening" or "Since many attendees are new believers, beware of questions requiring previous theological knowledge."

Meet with the Lead Team

Plan an outing with your lead team, maybe an overnight at a lake house or a cozy dinner at home. Build excitement for the ministry opportunities ahead and a community spirit. This gathering initiates the process and fosters creativity. Brainstorm the theme and solicit ways to use that theme in the largest decoration down to the smallest detail.

Include a time of praying and planning. If you allow each committee head to share her ideas, you'll find that the team encourages and inspires one another with new ideas and practical suggestions and resources. This meeting is the first domino in a steady stream that culminates in a life-changing retreat. Be sure to invite your speaker if she's local.

Plan Your Publicity

How will you inform women about the retreat? Who will package the publicity so that women will be excited about attending? Megachurches may offer staff publicity support. Publicizing your retreat looks much different in a small church.

In small churches you may write bulletin announcements and create a brochure on the computer. Publicity may be mostly word of mouth as women interact. With ready-to-order papers, attractive brochures can be produced this way. However, in large churches, a brochure on ready-to-order paper might not fly. Other ministries produce full-color professional pieces, and the women's ministry is under pressure to do the same.

Decide on your brochure design in plenty of time to produce it. A full-color brochure might require several months from the design phase to printing and mailing. Would your budget allow you to send a letter to the women in your church and follow up with a brochure later? You decide which method will be most effective with your women and complementary to your budget.

Plan bulletin announcements and discover deadlines so you can submit them early enough to insure a spot. Reserve an in-house registration site if necessary. Ask artistic women to design a retreat logo to use throughout the publicity so every publicity item is quickly recognizable. Good publicity can determine your turnout.

Touch Base with Your Retreat Site

This is a good time to check in with your retreat site manager and make sure all the paperwork is in order. Ask when the site management needs to know exact numbers and articulate your set-up needs. This might require another site visit now that you have a better sense of what the weekend will look like. How many rooms will you need for small groups? Is there enough seating? Audiovisual equipment? Bathroom facilities? Ladders or other equipment you will need to decorate?

What will the site provide, and what will women be asked to bring? This information is necessary when you send out your confirmation mailing to help women with preparation specifics. Some sites provide sheets, pillows, blankets, and soap. Others ask that attendees bring their own. At some sites, varied style rooms are supplied differently. Attention to detail means no one is left without necessities and shows your desire to make everyone as comfortable as possible.

Determine Your Registration Procedure

Will you register the women at the church, through the mail, or online? In-house registration is the simplest, requiring women to fill out a form and pay at the same time. IBC found a triplicate form beneficial, retaining a copy for the coordinator and another for the registration coordinator, with the third form going to the registrant.

The form should include contact information, roommate and housing preference, and T-shirt size (if you are providing T-shirts). We have provided a sample form in appendix B. Remember that if your form needs to be printed, allow plenty of time.

If there is limited space at your retreat site, you may want to register women through the mail. That way everyone receives the form at the same time and has the same opportunity to fill it out and send it in. Ask women rooming together to send in their forms and money together in the same envelope to make this method simpler for the registration coordinator.

Online registration is the wave of the future and especially appreciated by computer jocks. However, we recommend that you use this as a supplementary method because not all women have computers and know how to use them to register. You'd hate to leave behind women who may have much to offer, despite their lack of technical savvy. If you plan online registration, recruit a woman skilled at setting up a site or web page and test it to be sure it is user friendly. Decide who will retrieve these registrations and how they will be processed.

This is also the time to determine your scholarship policy and procedure. See appendix C for a sample scholarship form.

Make Plans to Set a Special Atmosphere

Women invest countless hours and dollars creating space where they live. That atmosphere breeds acceptance, beauty, and an intangible ethos that draws family and friends back again and again to experience a special sense of belonging and love. How can you set that kind of atmosphere for your retreat? Of course, you can't spend the hours and dollars that women invest in their homes, but you can make the environment memorable, warm, and fun. Plan your decorations now and challenge your team to be on the alert to help you find what you need. Send them on a "search and research" mission. Areas to decorate include the retreat site entry, the outside grounds, entry to the main room as well as the main room itself, and the registration and hospitality areas.

If you need quilts to decorate the walls, get the word out. If your budget is small, ask women to scour local businesses for donations. If your serendipity team wants to give each woman a piece of jewelry as a remembrance, alert your bargain shoppers. It's amazing what these women can scout out given enough time. The atmosphere communicates how much you care.

Recruit for the Talent Show

This is one option for an evening event and an opportunity for women to show off their hidden talents. A talent show gives women the chance to do something a little crazy and "out of the box." You'll be amazed at the abilities of women in your church, and they will love the chance to try something different. Begin contacting women you think might be interested and let them consider joining together with friends or performing solo.

Locate a Promotional Gift Company

T-shirts with the retreat logo add fun to the weekend and help women feel a part of the group. It's fun too for everyone to dress in their matching T-shirts at least one day of the retreat. You may prefer a tote bag or water bottle instead. If you plan this special touch, identify a company and determine what the items will cost and who will do the design. Investigate deadlines so you can have T-shirts ready in the appropriate sizes.

Three Months Out

Subcommittees Meet

Instruct your team leaders to recruit a team to share the load and enjoy the harvest. Train your leaders to gather their teams periodically for accountability and encouragement. The program team is writing scripts for interrupts, researching games for after-hours fun, and recruiting actors for dramas. If you want to make a video as part of the drama, it will require beginning now. The breakout workshop coordinator is recruiting speakers, making sure she has a mix of topics.

This is the time the team leader can ask, "How's it going?" and "How can I help?" An effective retreat coordinator participates in some of these sub-committee meetings to discern which leaders need help and who can work independently. The workers also appreciate the coordinator's participation in painting decorations and sewing tote bags, giving them a sense that "nothing is beneath her" and that she is interested in getting to know them. These visits also help the retreat coordinator spy out great recruits for next year's lead team.

Implement Your Publicity

It's time to get the word out. Blanket your church with the exciting news and get women talking and encouraging each other to attend.

Plan the Registration Details

Determine your registration deadline and publicize it. Many women will be persuaded to honor that deadline, helping you to know numbers and needed information. However, in our experience, some women will want to register the day before. Do you turn them away? We don't, believing that these often undisciplined women or women with last-minutes changes need to be there. It could be that through hearing God's Word they become more considerate of others and less last minute in their planning. Some might say we are fostering their irresponsibility. You'll have to decide for yourself.

What kind of set-up will you need if you register in-house? A table will work, although you might spice up the setting with a large poster of the retreat site or a publicity piece that draws eyes and interest. Be sure to man the booth with friendly, informed workers to answer questions and promote enthusiasm. Choose a place that is easily seen and accessed. If you plan to create a pictorial section in your retreat notebook, take women's photos when they register.

How will you register large groups? Set up multiple tables supplied with forms, pens, and lots of energetic helpers. And provide multiple registration times, before and after church services, Bible studies, or other events. Make it quick and easy to register for "customer satisfaction."

Identify the Talent Show Acts

It's time to finalize who will perform in the talent show. The talent show coordinator needs to gently audition each potential act to determine if it fits the theme and whether it needs help. We don't want anyone to embarrass themselves at the retreat. Often the coordinator can make suggestions to strengthen the performance if needed.

Design Your Promotional Items

By now you should have decided on the retreat logo. Will you provide T-shirts, a tote bag for the women's notebooks, or perhaps a water bottle? Other ideas? Now is the time to make your choice(s) and communicate with your promotional company. Again, roll this expense into your retreat budget.

Select and Acquire Special Gifts

Decide what the gifts will be—usually they will complement your theme. Have your serendipity team purchase materials or place orders, keeping the budget and calendar in mind.

Two Months Out

Recruit an Army of Volunteers

Many hands make light work. Enlist women to help before, during, and after the retreat. No one will be overburdened, and you will help women enjoy a sense of ownership in the ministry. Where do you find volunteers? You can list your team coordinators' names on your brochure with e-mail or telephone numbers. Let interested women make a direct connection. Ask for help at women's Bible studies. Encourage women to recruit their friends.

Design and Produce Decorations

Now it's time to put your artists, seamstresses, and woodsmiths to work. It's exciting to see these teams emerge. Suddenly garages become workshops full of creative women covered in sawdust, paint, and Styrofoam, sharing stories and making memories. They borrow or rent trucks to transport their creations and arrive at the retreat site beaming like proud parents. Make sure their creations come apart and can be easily transported and set up.

Begin Registration

You will need a two-month window in a large church. However, in smaller churches you can wait until a month ahead.

Plan "Grazing" Food

Now is the time for the hospitality team to order snacks, desserts, extra drinks, and the like. Add to the fun by choosing theme-related items if possible. You should know your numbers in order to purchase large quantities from wholesale food distributors such as Sam's or Cisco.

Plan and Produce the Talent Show

The coordinator should schedule each act, considering the order and communicating with participants. The whole show should not run over an hour and should be carefully coordinated to enhance its effectiveness. It's a good idea for the coordinator to stay in touch with participants and help them work out details. She should also schedule rehearsals for a week or two before the retreat and on-site.

Solicit Information for the Notebooks

Contact church leaders in the women's, children's, and missions ministries. They may want to inform women of upcoming opportunities to serve or learn. Ask them to provide you with copy-ready material. Do you want to include a letter from your senior pastor, women's director, or retreat coordinator? Contact them and give them deadlines.

Arrange for Special Needs

Make your retreat accessible to everyone. This means you may need to rent golf carts for transporting women who struggle to walk long distances. These carts also come in handy when the retreat team needs to get from one end of the camp to the other quickly. Check the yellow pages or online for golf cart rentals and build the cost into your budget. Are special needs rooms available at the site? Be prepared for women who call with special needs.

Pray, Pray, Pray

By now the prayer coordinator has the names of the women who will be attending. Send these names to your prayer team and ask them to pray daily for each woman by name as well as for any other needs of the team.

Recruit Small Group Leaders

Who will facilitate small groups that welcome women and foster intimacy? Draw on Bible study leadership and others who have been trained to lead small groups. If needed, provide your own training. Much of the individual attention occurs during small groups, so it is mandatory to find skilled leaders who genuinely care and who have experience or expertise with wounded women. Enlist lay counselors to help with extreme cases.

Build in a "Ministry Mentality"

Throughout the weeks before the retreat, sensitize your team to the fact that they are called to minister to women. Their role is not simply to enjoy themselves, although you hope they will. Their role is to be alert to women who are new, alone, or may feel marginalized. Train your team not to sit with their friends but to sit with strangers, initiating a relationship and doing everything they can to connect these women to others and to the Lord. This "ministry mentality" is contagious. Soon you will notice other women reaching out. You have set an atmosphere where the Holy Spirit will orchestrate amazing "coincidences" that will draw nonbelievers and change lives.

Countdown

Before you head out to the retreat site, remember to:

- get a final count and communicate the numbers to the retreat site manager
- send out confirmation letters with room assignments, a list of what to bring, an agenda, a map, and emergency numbers (see appendix D)
- package all gifts and prepare for transport
- complete decorations and prepare for transport
- pick up your promotional items (T-shirts, bags, bottles)
- make name tags and luggage tags to attach to the tote bags
- assign women to small groups
- touch base with all coordinators to wrap up any last minute details
- purchase and prepare food for transport
- produce and assemble notebooks
- rehearse, rehearse, rehearse
- pray, pray, pray
- if your team plans to go to the retreat site early, secure accommodations

On-Site Countdown

Once you reach the retreat site, remember to:

- connect with the on-site manager
- display decorations

- set up registration table
- assign greeters at multiple entry points
- rehearse on-site
- check out site set up and audiovisual equipment
- plan prayer times
- give out T-shirts for coordinators to wear as they greet women
- secure emergency information and master keys

Part 2

Presenting . . .

*O*ver the next five chapters we share five retreat themes that we have used in our churches. You are welcome to use any of the themes, scripts, and "how to" instructions and may duplicate the scripts for use in your church. However, our hope is that after you borrow from us for a while, you will then take your team through the entire process of creating your own retreat themes. If you are a smaller church, you may choose less elaborate decorations and entertainment but you will still benefit from choosing a theme to make each retreat distinctive and memorable. It's all about degree—and the choice is all yours.

How can you create an atmosphere that will bring the theme to life? Begin with the main room and then consider how to decorate the registration area and maybe even the entrance to the site. Enlist women who love to decorate and let them go at it.

We delight in helping you, but we know that producing your own ideas will be more fun and fulfilling for everyone. God has endowed your women with creative gifts, and we encourage you to tweak these chapters to fit your situation and setting. The following sample retreats were produced in megachurches with hundreds of women attending. The challenge for larger church settings is how to make each woman feel special and to draw them despite the size of the gathering. Smaller churches may not have the finances or people to execute all the ideas found in these chapters. Beginners may be overwhelmed by the magnitude of ideas, feeling discouraged that "we could never do all that!" Remember, you don't have to! We are giving you an abundance of resources and you can pick and choose what will work best for you. Remember, the goal is to provide plenty of time for the women to rest, relax, and reflect—to "be still and know that [He is] God" (Ps. 46:10).

Chapter 7

Country Western

*T*his is a great starter theme because it is simple, easy, and cheap, at least in the Southwest. It also sets a down-home, relaxed atmosphere that puts everyone at ease. Collect bandanas to add a flare of inexpensive color. Suspend silver die-cut stars from the ceiling and paint the backs of them with glow-in-the-dark paint for an added surprise. Decorate with boots, bales of hay, lanterns, saddles, and scarecrows. Ask the women to don their western apparel or at least blue jeans and swing their partners in a rollicking square dance. Take a hayride or make s'mores over a campfire and consider calling your small group leaders "posse leaders."

If you want to go all out, gather or construct more elaborate settings like a life-size stagecoach, cut out wooden cows, or tack large swathes of bandana fabric around the ceiling in a scalloped pattern. We transformed a phone booth into an outhouse using a refrigerator box, and we borrowed a rancher's surrey, giving women the experience of the old West's most elegant means of transportation. The sheriff rode in on her stick horse to emcee an indoor rodeo on Saturday night. Find instructions for decorations, gifts, and games below.

Decorations

The stage itself was very simple. The back was draped in black fabric suspended on rods; red bandana fabric hung on either side and scalloped across the top. Larger silver cut-out stars hung randomly over the stage.

To enter the main room the ladies walked through a stagecoach. Follow these instructions to construct your own stagecoach.

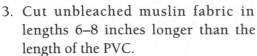

1. Place long tables four to six feet apart.
2. Attach four 1-inch PVC pipes cut at lengths to the outer edge of the tables, at even intervals. This forms an archway over the tables.
3. Cut unbleached muslin fabric in lengths 6–8 inches longer than the length of the PVC.
4. Measure the length of your tables, then add 4 feet times 2 for the overhang that will be gathered in later at each end, plus 3 inches for each PVC pipe that you are using. In other words, if you had 8-foot tables and four PVC pipes, then your measurement would be 17 feet. This measurement would determine how many lengths of muslin you would need to cut and sew together to be wide enough to go over the PVC to form the fabric part of the stagecoach. Muslin comes in many widths, so calculate which width would be your best buy and possibly the least number of pieces to have to sew together.
5. Sew 2-inch casings on either end of the fabric.
6. Now measure three feet from one sewn edge and sew a 2-inch casing. Repeat this at even intervals to match the spacing of your PVC pipes.
7. Slip the PVC through the four center casings and reattach to the table.
8. Run elastic through the end casings and secure ends to the inside edges of the table. That completes the top portion of your stagecoach.
9. Around the outer edge of the tables attach 18-inch-wide corrugated paper that looks like wood planks.
10. Find four old wagon wheels to lean against the tables or make them out of cardboard or wood and paint to look authentic.

You can cover the tables in red bandana fabric and display the ladies' name tags there as they enter. Make name tags with die-cut silver boots and red die-cut cowboy hats or any other western memorabilia.

You can achieve a similar stagecoach effect by painting a flat scene on several sheets of 4 by 8-foot insulation foam and cutting out the inside for the women to walk through. Anything western sitting around will also add to the atmosphere.

At a retreat in Detroit the room had mauve-colored, pinch-pleated curtains that clashed greatly with the red western decor, so we unhooked the curtains, turned them around, and rehooked them. The white lining complemented the red bandana fabric much better. We also cut large squares of bandana to tie around the backs of the chairs, giving the room a festive look.

Always ask some of your local schools and churches if they have things that you can use. You will be amazed how God will supply.

Suggested Activity Schedule

Friday: **Session One**
hayride, bonfire, surrey ride, etc.
Saturday: **Session Two**
free time and breakout sessions
Session Three
indoor rodeo
Sunday: **Session Four**
worship service

Publicity Logo

Ask an artist in your congregation to draw a western scene or pull something off the Internet. We used two boots with a bandana tied around them to advertise the retreat. Any western paraphernalia will work great to help promote the weekend.

Special Gift Ideas

Use your imagination. A woman in our church sewed little drawstring bandana bags to package the retreat gifts. It is fairly easy to find western sacks or even use brown paper bags folded over and tied with red raffia. Our gift that year was silver rings with a cross cut out in them.

Drama and "Interrupts"

The scripts below, and in each of the next four chapters, were written and produced by Karen Black, a talented writer and actress. Karen has used her dramatic gifts and great sense of humor to break down walls of resistance and prepare women to hear from God at IBC retreats. Need a script consultant? Contact Karen at kblack@newdoors.info.

Country Western Session One Script

Background: The retreat coordinator normally opens the first session with a general welcome, introduction of special guests, explanation of the schedule for the weekend, and any other important announcements. For the purpose of this example, the emcee is Jo Ann, affectionately referred to as "Miz Jonesy." The Sheriff is dressed in full western wear, including cowboy hat, boots, and possibly holster and cap gun. Suggestions for theme music are "Rawhide," "Bonanza," or Aaron Copland's "Rodeo—Hoe-Down." The retreat group is divided into several teams with no more than fifty women per team. A team captain, or "deputy," is selected for each team before the retreat and given an idea of her responsibilities. In this example, the deputies are Miz Suzy and Miz Lisa.

JO ANN: I am so excited this weekend is finally here! I thought that the best way to get this started was to bring up the planning team. So please join me in welcoming the retreat committee *[introduce several members]* and the Fun and Games Director, Karen. *[She appears to not be in the room.]*

Maybe she didn't hear me. Once again . . . Karen! *[nothing happens]* What is going on? I don't believe this! After all our hard work, she doesn't even bother to show up. I demand an explanation!

SOUND TECH: *[start western music and continue until Sheriff reaches front]*

SHERIFF: *[This is the missing Karen in disguise, moseying up front.]* Well, Miz Jonesy, I'm afraid I've got some mighty bad news for you.

JO ANN: It's Jo Ann. Who are you, and what in the world are you doing dressed in that get-up?

SHERIFF: Excuse me. This ain't no get-up. This is the way we all dress down in Texas where I come from. And we ride our horses to work and pump oil right in our back yards! I dun rode herd on a big cattle drive all the way from Texas, and I got me a mess a cows out here with no cowpokes to hep me round 'em up!

JO ANN: *[agitated]* What do you mean, cowpokes?

SHERIFF: Now settle yerself down, Miz Jonesy.

JO ANN: It's JO ANN!

SHERIFF: Uh-huh . . . whatever. Well, like I was saying, Miz Jonesy, I got me a real calamity on my hands!

JO ANN: Calamity! I don't care about your calamity—I'm having one right now!

SHERIFF: Uh-huh . . . whatever. Like I was sayin', I got me a real calamity on my hands. I was herding a bunch of cattle out this direction and, by golly, somehow them cows got loose!

JO ANN: What do you mean, some cows are loose?

SHERIFF: Well, Miz Jonesy, there's cows runnin' loose all over this here campground! You might of seen some of them—look, there's one now!

[Someone runs through with wooden cow.]

JO ANN: You're right, Sheriff! Those cows are everywhere! They are going to ruin this retreat!

SHERIFF: Now we're in fer it! We're gonna have to git us some hep roundin' up all them cows before you can even think about retreatin'!

[continues] Here's what we're gonna do. I need me a few deputies to hep round up them cows. Miz Suzy and Miz Lisa, come on up here! *[Call up all deputies and put sheriff stars on them.]* I am here and now deputizin' all you lovely ladies out here to help us round up all them cows and go on a cattle drive to herd them back to Fort Worth. Please stand and raise yer right hand and repeat after me. *[If you choose to use a cap gun and holster, the sheriff takes out her gun and places it over her heart.]* "I do solemnly swear" . . . (oh, I know, you purty ladies don't swear) . . . "I promise to do everything the Sheriff or Miz Jonesy or Miz Suzy or Miz Lisa sez to do." That'll do. Now put your arms down, you're killin' me!

Jo Ann: If'n you look on your name tag, you can find a number, and we're gonna tell you which posse you are going to be a part of. We are going to divide up into posses to help round up these cows.

Sheriff: If'n your number is one through four, follow Miz Suzy to that corner of the room. Five through eight follow Miz Lisa to that corner. Once you git in your corner, yer goin' to come up with a fancy western name for yer posse, make sure you know all yer fellow posse members, and put together an inspirational cheer to encourage your posse to round up them cows! Ready—go!

Sound Tech: *[Play western music softly while groups are meeting.]*

[Note: Depending on how large the groups are, give them enough time to meet some new people, get somewhat organized, and prepare to perform their cheer. The Sheriff then calls up the teams one at a time, and they announce their new posse name and then perform their cheer.]

Country Western Session Two Script

Jo Ann: Welcome back, cowgirls. I trust you had a good night's sleep. Or maybe you stayed up really late getting to know the other ladies in your room. Isn't it fun to have a good old-fashioned slumber party once in a while? I hope you are ready for an exciting day as we continue to fellowship together, study God's Word, and even have some fun, Texas style! I have seen a few of those missing cows running around our camp this morning, so let's bring up our Sheriff and find out if she's having any success rounding them up!

Sound Tech: *[Play western theme until Sheriff gets up front.]*

Sheriff: Mornin', Miz Jonesy! How y'all doin'?

Jo Ann: It's JO ANN!

Sheriff: Uh-huh . . . whatever. Well, Miz Jonesy, I ain't havin' much success roundin' up them cows. Ah'm gonna need me some hep.

JO ANN: Well, Sheriff, I tried calling some of those cows over, and they didn't seem to pay me any attention.

SHERIFF: How'd you holler at them?

JO ANN: I said, "Hello, cows! Please head back to the corral."

SHERIFF: Well, Miz Jonesy, that right there is the problem. Them cows ain't gonna answer if you talk at 'em like that! You got to speak "Texan" so they can understand ya!

JO ANN: Speak "Texan"? Why, whatever do you mean?

SHERIFF: Have mercy! We gonna have to have a trainin' session so you purty ladies can hep me round up them cows! Who you got in this crowd with the furtherest thing from a good old Texas accent you can get?

JO ANN: Well, ladies, who sounds the least like a Texan?

[**Note:** *You can take suggestions from the crowd or privately have selected someone with a very prim and proper attitude and accent. This was most successful with an exchange student from Jamaica at a Dallas Theological Seminary women's retreat.*]

[*Once the selection is made, bring her up to the stage and "initiate" her as an honorary Texan by putting a bandana around her neck and a cowboy hat on her head. Use the following "That's right, you're not from Texas" script with her reading from the first column using her normal accent, and then the Sheriff "correcting" her with the second column in her best "Texas" accent. Then she tries to repeat the Sheriff's line with a Texas accent.*]

SOUND TECH: [*Once the skit is concluded, play Lyle Lovett's "That's Right, You're Not from Texas" as the Sheriff and "new Texan" leave the stage.*]

That's Right, You're Not from Texas!

Hello	Howdy
I'm from Detroit (DEE-TROIT).	Ah'm from the Lone Star State.
President Bush	Dubya
Is it time for lunch?	Ah'm fearsome hungry.
Shall I fix you something to eat?	Ah'm gonna rustle up sum grub.
What's this chunky soup?	How long has it been since you had a hot steamin' bowl of wolf-brand chili? Well, that's too long!
I'm tired.	Ah'm plum tuckered out!
The animals have escaped!	Them cows done busted thru my barbwire fence!
It's time.	Ah'm fixin' to start thinkin' about it.
Ford, Chrysler, General Motors—the big three	A big old Caddy with a pair of longhorns as a hood ornament
It gets cold up here.	If'n a blue norther blows through threatenin' snow, we close the schools!
You lose 90 percent of your body heat through your head.	Whar's my Stetson?
I hate my hair!	Just rat it up and make it big!
Let's walk to the car.	Just mosey on over.
I don't recall.	Ah done fergit more than ah ever member.

Don't raise your voice to me!	Ah ain't hollerin'!
How much does this cost?	You want that in silver dollars or black gold?
My water bed is leaking.	Dad gum it, ah forgot to take off them spurs again!
Can you join us for dinner some evening?	Ya'll come on over for a mess of barbecue tonight.
Are these pickles?	Them jalapeño peppers ain't worth nuthin' unless you break into a sweat.
Detroit	Big D little a double l A S (Dallas)
Why does it have a hole in the roof?	So God can watch his team!
I'm leaving now.	Ah'm gone.
Good-bye.	Ya'll come back now, ya hear!

Country Western Session Three Script

JO ANN: Welcome back, ladies. What a great day this has been! *[Review the day's activities.]* And we have a great evening planned for you as well. I'm almost afraid to say this, but, come on back up here, Sheriff, and clue us in on what you have planned for tonight.

SOUND TECH: *[Play western theme until Sheriff gets up front.]*

SHERIFF: Evenin', Miz Jonesy! How y'all doin'?

JO ANN: I give up. I'm starting to get used to the whole "Miz Jonesy" thing!

SHERIFF: Uh-huh . . . whatever. Well, Miz Jonesy, ah'm afeard y'all are gonna have to git really serious about roundin' up them cows, 'cause ah'm needin' to get myself back to Texas powerful soon!

JO ANN: Oh dear. What are you going to make us do now?

SHERIFF: Now settle yerself down, Miz Jonesy! It ain't nothin' to be sceered about!

JO ANN: "Sceered" doesn't begin to cover it!

SHERIFF: All ah'm gonna need is for all you purty ladies to git yerselves all dressed up in yer very best Texan attire and git yerselves back up here after small groups for a genuine Texas round-em-up rodeo!

JO ANN: You have *got* to be kidding! There aren't any rodeo grounds around here!

SHERIFF: Oh, don't you git yer pretty head all riled up, Miz Jonesy! I got all them contingencies figgered out! You jist make sure all these ladies got their bandannas, Stetsons, boots, and spurs on tonight! Ah'm gonna mosey on out of here and start roundin' up the horses, saddles, and bulls!

JO ANN: What about the rodeo clowns?

SHERIFF: Well, Miz Jonesy, I think you done got that one covered! Ah'm gone! Y'all come back now, ya hear!

SOUND TECH: *[Play western theme until Sheriff makes her exit.]*

Special Events and Games

This theme lends itself to a variety of fun activities—a hayride, bonfire, surrey ride, or a fun-packed evening of games—an indoor rodeo!

Introduction to Rodeo

JO ANN: Well, what a great evening. I don't know about you, but it's past my bedtime and I'm ready to hit the hay!

SOUND TECH: *[Start western music and continue until Sheriff reaches the stage.]*

SHERIFF: *[moseys up front]* Well, Miz Jonesy . . .

JO ANN: It's JO ANN!

SHERIFF: Uh-huh . . . whatever. These authentic cowpokes don't look tired to me! You can't go to bed now—we're just gettin' started! We got to git ready to round up all them cows! Deputies, y'all come on up here and let's organize us a real Texas rodeo! *[Hopefully, there will be cheering from the crowd!]*

[continues] Here's what we're gonna do. Miz Suzy and Miz Lisa, you take these here sheets and git yer posses organized. 'Cause in about ten minutes, we're gittin' this hootin' and hollerin' rodeo under way! Yee ha!

Rodeo Events

Divide into posses and give time for deputies to recruit participants for each suggested rodeo event.

1. *Barrel Race:* Each team has four riders who ride stick horse at a gallop (with end of stick remaining on ground at all times) around one trash can and then the other, then race back to starting line.
2. *Target Practice:* Shooter fires water pistol at shaving cream on target's nose.
3. *Bucket Brigade:* Each team has four riders and eight horses. Two horses at a time hold hands and form a saddle to carry rider. Rider fills cup with water, mounts, and horses carry rider to other end. Rider cannot cover cup with hand. Rider stays on horse and pours cup into bucket at other end. Horse and rider race back to start, dismount, and pass empty cup to next rider. Continues with rider/horse teams until time is called, so each horse and rider team may go several times. Winner is team with most water poured into bucket at the end.

4. *Dizzy Lizzie:* Each team has four riders, two riders at each end of room. Each rider takes a stick horse, places her head on top of the horse's head, and spins around ten times. End of stick horse must remain on ground. Rider then drops the horse and runs to the other end and tags next runner, who repeats the game. (Important note: Have all team members not participating in this event form a protective barrier around the room. Dizzy Lizzie riders will get *very* dizzy, so be prepared to catch them.)

5. *Herding Dogies:* Entire team participates. Select four of the most petite women to be the "dogies". Everyone else sits on the floor, side by side with legs stretched out, alternating the direction they are facing so that one woman's feet are beside the next woman's hips and so on. Get into as tight a row as possible, with arms extended and palms facing up (this forms the "river"). The dogies (two at each end) are then passed down the river one at a time. If a dogie falls to the ground, she has to return to beginning of the river and start over.

Conclude the evening with either square dancing or line dancing to country music. This really is fun for women who don't get chances to dance very often.

Chapter 8

Patterns of Life

There is no place like home! This theme captures that warm, comforting glow of home that makes women feel secure and loved. It is simple to execute, giving many women opportunities to participate. Call for quilts and hang them around your meeting rooms. Ask each contributor to write the history of the quilt or an interesting story about its maker and display it on a card under the quilt. Decorate the stage like grandma's attic. Use quilted material to border your name tags and tote bags. Your quilters and seamstresses will be an invaluable resource to help bring this theme to life.

Add bees to the mix for fun and lots of laughter. How do bees fit the theme? Haven't you heard of a quilting bee? Check out the scripts below for the antics of our four-bee team: Queen Bee, Quilting Bee, Spelling Bee, and Busy Bee. Dress them in yellow and black bee costumes and decorate the stage with a 7-foot hive for a buzzing good time.

Decorations

Find a 5-foot-in-diameter round cylinder to use as the base of the beehive. Cut openings on either side for the bees to come in and out. Take chicken wire that is quite a bit longer than the circumference of the cylinder, gather it in, and staple it to the bottom edge of the cylinder. Gather the wire at the top and staple it to the cylinder, forming a large bubble or tube around the base. Continue layering rows of wire to the top of the cylinder. Form a dome-shaped top with the chicken wire to complete the top portion of the hive. You will crimp the chicken wire in at different intervals to give it that hive look.

Soak inexpensive unbleached muslin in a solution that is one part glue and two parts water (or you can buy ready-made fabric glue at your local craft store) and drape it around the chicken wire. At this point you puff and play with the fabric to get the kind of look you want. After that dries thoroughly, paint it a golden yellow and then give it some texture by shading it with different hues of brown. Glue a 1½-inch thick rope in the crevasses to make it look more authentic. The finished product will be about seven feet tall.

To make the hive look as if it is hanging on a tree, crinkle brown paper around tubes, add a few green leaves, and adhere it all to the hive. One of our creative art teachers made 12-inch diameter bees out of papier-mâché to sit on the hive. On the other side of the stage we placed a tall arched trellis with a swing hanging from it. All around the room we hung quilts with large paper clamps. Placed around the camp were 4 by 4-foot wooden bee cut-outs.

Two women from the church made a 10 by 7-foot cross quilt that we suspended on the stage Sunday morning. Many churches have borrowed the quilt for their special events over the years.

For name tags, we used the same fabric that was in the quilt. Yardage was machine quilted and cut into rectangles with pinking shears. We found computer printable sheets of unbleached muslin at a craft store, printed the attendees' names onto the muslin, then cut them out and sewed them onto the quilted rectangle.

A smaller church used this same theme, and their hive was made from inexpensive rolls of brown paint paper (found in the paint department of your local hardware store). It was crinkled up and hot glued in a spiral effect around a small dome tent. A little paint for texture, a paper tree limb, and this had a great look to it.

Suggested Activity Schedule

Friday: **Session One**
                royal ball and community activities

Saturday: **Session Two**
                free time and breakout sessions
                Session Three
                "Patterns of Our Lives" melodrama/talent show

Sunday: **Session Four**
                worship service

Publicity Logo

Notebook covers, posters, and brochures looked like patchwork quilts with pictures of past retreats in some of the patches. You can drape your registration table with quilts and hang quilts around the church to create excitement about the upcoming weekend together.

Special Gifts Ideas

Suggested special gifts include matted copies of the Weaver's Prayer (see below). Consider also small devotional books with quilt art.

The Weaver's Prayer

My life is but a weaving between my Lord and me
I cannot see the colors He worketh steadily.
Oft times He weaveth sorrow and I in foolish pride
Forget He sees the upper and I the underside.

Not till the looms are silent and the shuttles cease to fly
Shall God unroll the canvas and explain the reason why.
The dark threads are as needful in the Weaver's skillful hands
As the threads of gold and silver in the pattern He has planned.

—Anonymous

Drama and "Interrupts"

Patterns of Life Session One Script

Background: All of our bee characters were in full costume, including wings and antennae. The Queen Bee also had a tiara and a scepter. The musical introduction song was a simple jazz tune, which is included at the end of the first session interrupt. The three worker bees were hidden in a large beehive on the stage and came out during the first chorus of the song.

EMCEE: I am so excited about this weekend. When we came up with the idea of using quilting and God's patterns in our lives as our theme, we wanted to incorporate quilts into our decorations as well. I especially want to thank those of you who contributed quilts with their own special stories for us to display this weekend. Ladies, please take time to walk around and read the histories of these quilts sometime during the weekend. Because so many of them are quite old and fragile, please don't touch the quilts. We will all just enjoy them from afar. So, getting back to our plans for this weekend, I have asked our Retreat Program Director, Karen, to come up with some creative ways to use quilts this weekend. So let's welcome her and see what she has in mind.

SOUND TECH: *[Introductory music, "Flight of the Bumblebee" by Rachmaninoff.]*

[Queen Bee enters from back of room tossing Bit 'O Honey candy to crowd.]

EMCEE: What on earth is going on?

QUEEN BEE: I'm here, baby, and I'm ready to go!

EMCEE: Why are you dressed up in that ridiculous outfit?

QUEEN BEE: I beg your pardon! I am dressed appropriately for this weekend, just like you told me!

EMCEE: I *never* told you to dress like that!

QUEEN BEE: I am just following your lead, putting together all the fun and games to tie in with the theme of this retreat.

EMCEE: I'm not sure what you are dressed as, but that has *nothing* to do with quilts!

QUEEN BEE: Quilts? You didn't say anything to me about quilts!

EMCEE: I specifically told you that the theme for this retreat was "Patterns of Life" and that we were using quilts.

QUEEN BEE: You did? You're sure you said quilts?

EMCEE: Yes, *hello*, it's quilts! This is unbelievable! You've ruined the whole thing! Why are you dressed up like that—who or *what* do you think you are?

QUEEN BEE: I'm the *Queen Bee*, baby! Buzzin' around this hive!

EMCEE: Of all the ridiculous things—what in the world does a *bee* have to do with quilts?

QUEEN BEE: You told me you were going to divide these women up into small groups like bees!

EMCEE: I said we could call the small groups "quilting bees," but that was about *quilts,* not *bees!* I told you we were decorating with quilts, setting up the stage as Grandma's sewing room, and that I wanted you to come up with some ideas revolving around that. What in the world were you thinking?

QUEEN BEE: I remember we were talking, and you were on your cell phone and I was on my C *Bee* radio, and we didn't really have a good connection. I didn't hear anything about quilts!

EMCEE: I can't believe this. I brought you all the way up here to help with this retreat, and you get it all messed up!

QUEEN BEE: *Oops!* Well, this is really embarrassing!

EMCEE: I don't *bee*lieve this! What are we going to do now?

QUEEN BEE: We're just gonna have to go with it. You just take a seat, and let me take it from here. They don't call me *Queen Bee* for nothing! Hit it! *[said to keyboard player who starts jazz music]*

Well, I'm the Queen Bee, baby
Buzzin' around this hive
I'm the Queen Bee, baby
Buzzin' around this hive
I can make honey, baby
Better than any bee that's alive

Yeah, I'm the Queen Bee, baby
These are my worker bees

[Worker bees now exit hive to begin singing their choruses.]

WORKER BEES: She's the Queen Bee, baby
               We're the worker bees

QUEEN BEE: I've got quilting, spelling, and busy
               They number 1—2—3

QUILTING BEE: I'm the Quilting Bee, baby
               I can stitch a quilt
               I'm the Quilting Bee, baby
               I can stitch your quilt
               I can piece and sew and batt and quilt
               I quilt to the hilt

SPELLING BEE: I'm the Spelling Bee, baby
               I can spell any word
               I'm the Spelling Bee, baby
               Spell any word that's occurred
               From ABC to XYZ
               Word by word, I'll be heard

BUSY BEE: I'm the Busy Bee, baby
               Busy all day long
               I'm a Busy Bee, baby
               Busy singin' this song
               I can buzz around from hive to hive
               Blink an eye, I'll be gone

QUEEN BEE: Yeah, I'm the Queen Bee, baby
               Come join my worker bees

WORKER BEES: She's the Queen Bee, baby
               Join us worker bees

QUEEN BEE: If you wanna buzz around this hive
               Buzz along with me
               Up on your feet, let's buzz *[motions to the crowd to get them
               up, and worker bees go out into the crowd to encourage every-
               one to buzz]*

EVERYBODY: Buzz Buzz Buzz Buzz
               Buzz Buzz Buzz Buzz

Buzz Buzz Buzz Buzz
Buzz Buzz Buzz Buzz

QUEEN BEE: Buzz it, Busy!

[Busy Bee plays kazoo]

QUEEN BEE: Yeah, I'm the Queen Bee, baby
You're buzzin' along with me

WORKER BEES: She's the Queen Bee, baby
You're buzzin' with 1—2—3

ALL: And we can make honey, baby
Better than any bee you'll ever see

And we can make honey, baby
Better than any bee you'll ever see

Oh yeah!

Patterns of Life Session Two Script

EMCEE: *[Welcome and announcements]*

SOUND TECH: *[Play "Flight of the Bumblebee."]*

[Entrance of Queen Bee and worker bees]

EMCEE: Oh no! Here they come again! Un*bee*lievable!

QUEEN BEE: Good morning, *[name of emcee]*! How have you *beeeen*?

EMCEE: Just fine until you showed up!

QUEEN BEE: Are your wings all in a tangle this morning? You must have been up all night dancing at the Royal Ball—or were you singing old *Beetle* tunes at karaoke?

QUILTING BEE: I think I saw her making a *bee*line for the Bunco tables.

SPELLING BEE: That's Bunco—B U N C O—Bunco.

BUSY BEE: I'm sure she was busy at the *bee*ngo hall! Did you win anything?

EMCEE: Just another stuffed animal to add to my *Bee*nie Baby collection!

QUEEN BEE: Everybody's got to get into the act!

EMCEE: What I would really like is for you to fly on out of here so we can get started with our morning session!

QUEEN BEE: Well, I'm insulted. As the Queen Bee, you'd think I would get some respect.

SPELLING BEE: R E S P E C T! *[sing like Aretha Franklin]* Respect.

EMCEE: Now, shoo! Get out of here before I get the bug spray! We're trying to *bee* spiritual here, and you bees just don't *bee*long!

QUILTING BEE: Why you old sew and sew!

SPELLING BEE: That's sew—S E W—sew.

QUEEN BEE: I'll have you know we bees are extremely spiritual.

EMCEE: You are out of your beeswax! How could bees *bee* spiritual?

BUSY BEE: Haven't you ever heard of the *Bee*atitudes?

SPELLING BEE: B E E A T I T U D E S—*Bee*atitudes.

QUEEN BEE: Okay, girls. Open your *Bee*bles. All bees who love the Bee-keeper know the *Bee*atitudes—and we try to live by them every day. God blesses the bees who realize their need for Him. The kingdom of heaven will *bee* given to them.

[Bees open their little "Beeble" booklets and read the "Beeatitudes."]

QUILTING BEE: God blesses the poor little bees who mourn, for they will *bee* comforted.

SPELLING BEE: God blesses the bees who are gentle and lowly, for the whole beehive will belong to them. Beehive—B E E H I V E—beehive.

BUSY BEE: God blesses those busy bees who are hungry and thirsty for justice, for justice will *bee* served in full.

QUEEN BEE: God blesses the bees who are merciful, for they will *bee* shown mercy.

QUILTING BEE: God blesses the bees whose hearts are full of pure honey, for they will see God.

SPELLING BEE: God blesses the peacekeeping bees, for they will *bee* called the children of the great Beekeeper. B E E K E E P E R—Beekeeper.

BUSY BEE: God blesses those bees that are swarmed because they live for God. The Great Beehive is theirs.

QUEEN BEE: And God blesses all His bees, even when they are mocked and swatted for buzzing after Him. *Bee* happy about it! For a great reward awaits us in heaven.

EMCEE: You guys are just the *bee's* knees!

[Bees bow and make their exit.]

Patterns of Life Session Three Script

EMCEE: *[Welcome and review of the day]*

SOUND TECH: *[Play "Flight of the Bumblebee."]*

[Enter Queen Bee and worker bees]

EMCEE: Oh no! We're being swarmed again!

QUEEN BEE: Hi, honey! How are you?

EMCEE: What have you bees *beee*en up to this afternoon?

QUILTING BEE: I spent all afternoon cutting and piecing at Creative Memories.

SPELLING BEE: Creative Memories—C R E A T I V E M E M O R I E S—Creative Memories.

BUSY BEE: I was buzzin' from the Frisbee golf, to miniature golf, to boot camp, and then to horseback riding. You should have seen that horse bolt when I gave him a little sting! Has that rider made it back to camp yet?

EMCEE: Wow—I feel guilty. All I did was take a nap!

QUEEN BEE: Oh, honey—you are really just a wanna*bee* aren't you?

QUILTING BEE: I know—let's just stitch her into this colony!

SPELLING BEE: She can join the royal hive—R O Y A L H I V E—royal hive.

BUSY BEE: Hurry up! Let's get busy and initiate her!

EMCEE: Oh no! I don't *bee*lieve this! What have I gotten myself into?

QUEEN BEE: This is an honor for you. You should *bee* buzzed!

EMCEE: That's what I'm afraid of.

QUILTING BEE: Here's your honorary antenna. *[puts antenna on Emcee]*

SPELLING BEE: And you need some *bee* sparkle dust. *[puts glitter on Emcee's cheeks]*

BUSY BEE: And you need some wings so you can buzz around this hive! *[puts wings on]*

QUEEN BEE: And now you are an official worker bee, honey!

EMCEE: Does that mean I get to *bee* a part of all the things you have planned for tonight?

SPELLING BEE: No—N O—no.

BUSY BEE: We have *bee*en so busy getting together a great lineup of options for you tonight—I can't wait!

QUEEN BEE: So after small groups, *bee* sure to come right back in here for an evening you will *bee* talking about for months! See you later—gotta buzz!

SOUND TECH: *[Play "Flight of the Bumblebee."]*

Special Events

To complement the theme of community, we filled the evening hours with community building activities, giving women multiple opportunities to connect. Ask women to bring old photographs of great grandmothers and other ancestors to share. Show women how to scrapbook to protect and display loved ones' future heritage.

The Queen Bee also hosted a Royal Ball on Friday night, and we performed a melodrama for Saturday night's entertainment. Below are the scripts for both events.

Introduction to the Queen Bee's Royal Ball Script

EMCEE: Well, I hope you enjoyed meeting some new women in your small group "quilting bees." You will get together again this weekend, and this provides a great opportunity to make new friendships. I hesitate to say this, but let's bring back our Queen Bee and her worker bees and hear what she has planned for us this evening.

SOUND TECH: *[Play "Flight of the Bumblebee."]*

              [Queen Bee and worker bees enter from back.]

QUEEN BEE: I am so excited—I'm just all abuzz!

QUILTING BEE: All the pieces of the pattern are starting to come together!

SPELLING BEE: Pattern—P A T T E R N—pattern.

BUSY BEE: I have been un*bee*lievably busy getting everything ready.

EMCEE: I'm afraid to ask, but what do you have planned?

QUEEN BEE: Oh, not just one thing, but 1—2—3 options!

QUILTING BEE: You are such a stitch! The number one option is the Queen Bee's Royal Ball! Right here, tonight!

QUEEN BEE: We'll be dancing until the bees come home!

SPELLING BEE: The second option is karaoke in the lounge. That's karaoke—K A R A O K E—karaoke.

BUSY BEE: Or for those of us who are too busy to settle on just one thing, you can buzz around to all the games like Bingo, Bunco, and Dominoes. We even have prizes!

QUILTING BEE: There are refreshments in the snack room—maybe even Beenie Weenies!

QUEEN BEE: In order to have plenty of room for my Royal Ball, I need you to gather up all your *bee*longings, pick up your chair, and move to the sides of the room.

BUSY BEE: Let's get busy!

*[**Note:** We put together a dance music CD with many different types of music. A suggested list is included below.]*

"Beat It"
"Chicken Dance"
"Conga"
"Cotton Eyed Joe"
"Dance to the Music"
"Footloose"
"Fun Fun Fun"
"Get on Your Feet"
"Get Ready 4 This"

"Great Balls of Fire"
"Hokey Pokey"
"I Want to Hold Your Hand"
"Joy to the World"
"Larger than Life"
"Let's Twist Again"
"Mac the Knife"
"Macarena"
"Man! I Feel Like a Woman!"
"Maniac"
"Na, Na, Hey, Hey, Good-bye"
"New York, New York"
"Respect"
"Rhythm Is Gonna Get You"
"Shout"
"Smooth"
"Some Days You Gotta Dance"
"Stayin' Alive"
"The Last Dance"
"We Are Family"
"What a Girl Wants"
"Wide Open Spaces"
"YMCA"
"[You Make Me Feel Like] A Natural Woman"
"You Make Me Feel Like Dancin'"

"The Patterns of Our Lives" Melodrama Script

Background: After the main session and small groups on Saturday night, the women were invited to return for an evening of entertainment. Earlier in the weekend, the retreat committee gathered names of women who might enjoy giving an impromptu performance on stage. The Queen Bee calls out the names of these women, and they go backstage, where they are given their scripts as well as costumes and props. The more outrageous the costumes, the better and funnier! Costumes need to include fancy dresses, boas, scarves, jewelry, hats, wigs, and anything else you can think of. Scripts are provided for each character with their lines and actions highlighted. A list of characters is included at the end of this script.

One of the funniest moments in the melodrama is the commercial break. This is a take-off on a popular commercial, but the twist that makes it absolutely hilarious is when you have previously arranged for several of the oldest women to perform the commercial. We have always gotten the biggest laughs when we use the most unexpected women for this joke.

During the organization of the melodrama backstage, the worker bees hold an "open mike" where any kind of song, poem, or joke using the theme of quilting or bees is encouraged. You will be surprised at the creativity and enthusiasm once people begin to get into the act. It is a good idea to plant some ideas in the crowd to encourage participation.

Once the melodrama players are ready, the Queen Bee calls for attention and serves as the narrator. Worker bees help keep people organized and distribute props as needed. It is essential that all characters be heard clearly.

SOUND TECH: *[Play "Days of Our Lives" theme.]*

NARRATOR: As stitches in a patchwork quilt, so are the patterns of our lives. Join us as we look in on a small, not-so-quiet town in middle America. As our scene opens, the town of Beeville is all abuzz. The matriarch of Beeville, Beeatrice Hive, is hosting the weekly Quilting Bee Society meeting. Let's listen in. . . .

[Bonnie Beesley, Becky Beevers, Babs Beebe, and Beelinda Hand come in from stage right and gather in cluster, gossiping.]

SOUND TECH: *[Play soap opera-type music.]*

BONNIE: Well, hello, Becky Beevers. Have you heard the latest? What a scandal!

BECKY: Tell me, Bonnie Beesley, what's the buzz? Look—here comes Babs Beebe.

BABS: You won't *bee*lieve it! Beelinda Hand—have you heard?

BEELINDA: Beeatrice Hive's oldest daughter, Honey, has run off!

BONNIE,
BECKY, BABS: Un*bee*lievable!

BECKY: Who'd she run off with?

BONNIE: That new guy in town, Dirk Dobber.

BABS: The one who drives that black and yellow *Beemer*?

BEELINDA: Shh . . . here comes Beeatrice.

[Beeatrice Hive enters stage left with maid closely behind, fanning her.]

SOUND TECH: *[Play dramatic music.]*

BEEATRICE: Oh my . . . Oh my . . . How can this *bee*? Beeves, I think I'm going to faint.

MAID: Try to calm down, Miz Beeatrice. Here, take some of this vitamin *Bee* complex, it will help to settle your nerves.

BEEATRICE: You know I'm allergic to that, Beeves! I break out in hives!

[Gossipers run over to comfort Beeatrice.]

BONNIE: Oh, you poor dear. What can we do to help?

BECKY: Is there someone we can call?

SOUND TECH: *[Play "Ghostbusters" theme.]*

BABS: I know, let's call your pastor, Pastor _____. He'll know what to do.

[Maid gets phone and holds it while Beelinda dials.]

BEELINDA: Hello, Libbee. *[Try to get your pastor's wife for this character.]* How are you?

[Libbee enters stage right with phone.]

LIBBEE: I'm fine. Am I late for the quilting bee?

BEELINDA: Oh, you won't *bee*lieve it. I have terrible news. Honey Hive has run off with Dirk Dobber, and Beeatrice is *bee*side herself!

[Libbee overreacts terribly.]

LIBBEE: How horrible! I will tell Pastor _____ to make a *bee*line over there to counsel her as soon as he finishes his one-on-one *Bee*ball tournament.

BEELINDA: Basketball again?

LIBBEE: You know he only works one day a week—Sunday. He has absolutely nothing else to do. *[Rolls eyes, hangs up phone, and exits.]*

[Aunt Bee and Uncle Ben enter from stage left.]

AUNT BEE: Oh, Beeatrice, my poor sister, how will you ever live down the shame?

UNCLE BEN: There's nothing like a good scandal to draw a family together. Where are the other girls?

NARRATOR: Our scene continues as Honey's sisters Shelbee, Colbee, Barbee, and Baybee enter *[from stage right]*.

SHELBEE: Aunt Bee, Uncle Ben, thank you for coming. But who's watching the candle factory?

UNCLE BEN: Don't worry, Shelbee, your cousin Wick, or as I call him, Dubya, is supervising the beeswax candle factory today.

AUNT BEE: I'm so worried about that boy. He hasn't been able to concentrate on the family *bee*sness since he hired that new secretary.

COLBEE: Uncle Ben, you hired a new secretary? I wanted that job!

BARBEE: Colbee, you know working with Cousin Wick would have only stirred up a hornet's nest—you two have never gotten along.

BAYBEE: I've never understood why Colbee and Wick can't stand to be in the same room together—you could cut the tension with a knife.

AUNT BEE: It all goes back to the fourth grade when Wick beat Colbee in the national spelling bee.

SHELBEE: Cousin Wick told me that he hired that blond hussy, Heather Lockerbee!

SOUND TECH: *[Play ominous music.]*

[Bonnie, Becky, Babs, and Beelinda run over to sisters.]

BONNIE: Girls, when did you realize your sister was missing?

SHELBEE: This morning when I went into her room to wake her up.

COLBEE: All her *beeautiful* clothes were gone!

BARBEE: There was only one thing left.

BONNIE,
BECKY, BABS,
BEELINDA: What was it?

BAYBEE: The only thing left was this *[holds up large comb]*—my *beeautiful* sister Honey's comb!

SOUND TECH: *[Play dramatic music.]*

NARRATOR: Now we must break for a commercial from our sponsor.

[Phone rings; Quilter 1 enters stage right wrapped in a quilt carrying a phone.]

QUILTER 1: Whassup?

[Quilter 2 enters stage left carrying a phone.]

QUILTER 2: Whassup?

QUILTER 1: Whassup?

QUILTER 2: Oh, nuthin, just piecing and quilting. Whassup with you?

QUILTER 1: Hold on, I'm getting beeeeeeped. Whassup?

QUILTER 3: Whassup?

QUILTER 1:   Whassup?

QUILTER 2:   Whassup?

NARRATOR: And now, back to our regularly scheduled program.

SOUND TECH: *[Play soap opera music.]*

NARRATOR: As our story continues, the scene changes to the local hospital—Beeville General.

[Emergency room nurse should be stationed at a desk.]

ER NURSE: Beeville General, please hold. Beeville General, please hold. Beeville General, please hold. *[opens compact and powders nose]*

[Paramedics, wearing yellow jackets, rush in carrying Honey, who is screaming. Dirk Dobber runs alongside.]

DIRK: We need a doctor! This woman is in un*bee*lievable pain!

ER NURSE: I'll be with you in a moment. *[continues to powder nose]*

PARAMEDIC 1:   Keep checking her vitals!

PARAMEDIC 2:   She's swelling up—we may lose her!

[Honey continues to scream.]

PARAMEDIC 1:   Do we need to perform CPR? *[to audience]* There's no way I'm doing mouth-to-mouth!

DIRK: You must save her! Where's the doctor! Hold on, Honey!

HONEY: *[swooning]* Dirk Dobber, you are the love of my life.

DIRK: *Bee* still my heart! Hang in there, Honey. Where's the doctor? Nurse, please help us!

ER NURSE: Before I can let you see the doctor, there are just a few questions I have to ask. Do you have insurance? What's your group number? Who's your primary care physician? Did you call for a referral?

PARAMEDIC 2: We don't have time for this now!

PARAMEDIC 1: This woman is swelling up like a *bee*hive!

PARAMEDIC 2: Nurse, let the forms *bee* for now—this woman may die!

ER NURSE: Just a few more questions—who will *bee* responsible for payment? Are you allergic to anything? Where did you get that lovely yellow jacket? Who does your hair? Are you related to the Hive sisters? Is that your black and yellow *Bee*mer? That's a hot car!

[Honey continues to scream.]

DIRK: That's my *Bee*mer convertible, and it is a hot car!

ER NURSE: *[flirting]* I'd love to take a ride some day. I'll give you my number, and you can give me a buzz.

PARAMEDIC 1: Nurse! The doctor please!

[Honey screams and passes out.]

ER NURSE: *[picks up phone]* Paging Dr. Feelgood. Dr. Feelgood to emergency—stat!

SOUND TECH: *[Play theme from "ER"]*

[Dr. Feelgood enters.]

DR. FEELGOOD: What seems to *bee* the problem here?

DIRK: We were running away to elope in the next town, Bee Valley, in my black and yellow *Bee*mer when my Honey suddenly screamed and collapsed. Doctor, can you save her?

DR. FEELGOOD: Is that your black and yellow *Bee*mer parked in my space? That's a hot car!

DIRK: Yes, it is. And I got an un*bee*lievable deal on it down at Beeville BMW.

[Enter Pastor _____ carrying basketball.]

PASTOR: Hello, Dr. Feelgood. I'm Pastor _____.

DR. FEELGOOD: Hello, Pastor _____. I see you play *Bee*ball. How about some one-on-one?

PASTOR: I would *bee* delighted. But what seems to *bee* the problem here?

DIRK: Pastor, Honey and I were on our way out of town when she suddenly screamed and collapsed. Please pray for her!

PASTOR: Aren't you that new guy in town, Dirk Dobber? Do you play *Bee*ball? Is that your black and yellow *Bee*mer? That's a hot car!

DIRK: Yes, it is.

DR. FEELGOOD: Excuuuuse me—but this patient may be dying!

*[Enter Beeatrice Hive, Shelbee, Colbee,
Barbee, Baybee, Aunt Bee, and Uncle Ben]*

BEEATRICE: Oh, Doctor! What is happening with my sweet Honey!

SHELBEE: Is she going to be all right?

COLBEE: She's swollen up like a *bee*hive!

BARBEE: If she dies, can I have her room?

BAYBEE: Can I have her clothes?

AUNT BEE: Girls, *bee*have!

UNCLE BEN: What do you think happened, doctor?

DR. FEELGOOD: Upon closer examination, I think Honey might have been stung by killer bees!

SOUND TECH: *[Play dramatic music.]*

[Beeatrice faints and is caught by Uncle Ben and fanned by Maid.]

[Enter Cousin Wick and new secretary, Heather Lockerbee.]

WICK: Mom, Dad, Aunt Beeatrice, Cousin Shelbee, Cousin Colbee, Cousin Barbee, Cousin Baybee—whew! Meet my new secretary, Heather Lockerbee.

SHELBEE: How dare you bring that hussy here!

COLBEE: Dubya, I demand that you fire her right now! I wanted that job!

WICK: Colbee, you couldn't tell a beeswax candle from a lamp post!

COLBEE: How dare you, Dubya!

[Colbee slaps Wick.]

HEATHER: Don't you slap him!

[Heather slaps Colbee. Everybody starts slapping everybody else. Beeatrice faints again.]

SOUND TECH: *[Play closing theme.]*

NARRATOR: And now a preview from tomorrow's episode of "Patterns of Our Lives." Honey is in a coma. Wick and Heather Lockerbee go to chapel to pray and light a beeswax candle for Honey. Fire breaks out at the Beeswax Factory, and that's just another normal day in Beeville.

Characters

Narrator (Queen Bee)
Beeatrice Hive
Daughters:
    Honey
    Shelbee
    Colbee
    Barbee
    Baybee
Dirk Dobber
Aunt Bee
Uncle Ben
Wick, their son
Libbee
Pastor _____
Dr. Feelgood
ER Nurse
Paramedic 1
Paramedic 2
Maid Beeves
Gossipers:
    Bonnie Beesley
    Becky Beevers
    Babs Beebe
    Beelinda Hand
Heather Lockerbee
Whassup quilters:
    Quilter 1
    Quilter 2
    Quilter 3

Chapter 9

Homecoming

*I*n an ideal world, we all would belong to a community of friends that loves and accepts us just as we are. Going home means reconnecting with loved ones and rehashing special memories. For believers, heaven will be like that. The Homecoming theme conjures up "school spirit" and a regathering of school chums that sets the scene for fun and spiritual renewal. Unleash your creative women and stand back as they transform the retreat site into memory lane.

We used paper mums as name tags, and the notebook was our school annual. Our school mascot was a cow—so we made life-sized wooden black and white spotted cows with big happy faces and placed them all around the site. We played up the cow theme everywhere—milk bottles in the dorms, "udder" cream as gifts, and a "cow" chorale choir. The cheerleaders, Muffy, Buffy, and Agnes, wore black and white cow print outfits. We borrowed a 14-foot, old-time school house from a decorating company and used it for registration. Megaphones, pom-poms, old retreat posters, and an old podium gave the main room the look of a high school gymnasium.

Everyone had a part in the homecoming parade: the student "cowncil;" the Cowbells pep squad; the Cow Chorale; and the band, playing kazoos and cowbells. At the Homecoming dance, the speaker was crowned the "Homecoming Dairy Queen."

We chose the cow as our mascot from the acronym "Christ Our Wonderful Savior." Borrow our cow theme or choose your own mascot and brainstorm ways to transform the site. Make this theme elaborate or simple. Below are instructions and ideas to prime the pump.

Decorations

This retreat took us all right back to those high school days of pep rallies, pom-poms, and parades. The main room was designed to look like a gymnasium or high school auditorium. We purchased many of our decorations from www.andersonsparty.com. A 12-foot-tall megaphone and 15-foot pom-poms certainly captured the homecoming theme we wanted. These simple kits from Anderson take the worry out of decorating but might challenge the engineering novice. Around the room we hung banners made of white butcher paper, but instead of the traditional game slogans we displayed the title and names of speakers of our past retreats. Twelve-foot-tall spirit ribbons draped both sides of the stage, declaring the speaker's name and message titles. We created a homecoming float out of a large refrigerator box, chicken wire, and squares of tissue paper. Two layers of the chicken wire were cut in cow shapes and mounted at the top of 1x4x6-foot boards. White and black 6-inch tissue squares were stuck in the wire to look like our cow, complete with pink udders. The boards were placed through the box and secured so it looked like the cow was standing on the box. Using the tissue squares, we hot-glued the center of the squares to the box and fluffed out the tissue. *Homecoming,* spelled out in die-cut letters, was fashioned on the outer edges of the box. We used cow-print fabric for registration tables and curtains and placed it throughout the camp to carry out the festive theme. Our greeters even wore cow-print vests for easy identification.

Suggested Activity Schedule

Friday: **Session One**
pep rally and bonfire, community activities
Saturday: **Session Two**
free time
Homecoming parade
Session Three
Homecoming dance
Sunday: **Session Four**
worship service

Publicity Logo

Our brochures, posters, and notebooks looked like the program for a homecoming weekend. We used cartoon cows and pictures of past retreats to invite women to join us for a weekend celebrating community.

Special Gifts Ideas

Beanie Babies were the craze that year. One of our committee heads donated Beanie Baby cows for each lady as a special treat. The ladies loved them. The gift that year was a silver bead bracelet with a dangling cross. We purchased them very reasonably at Shalina's, an international jewelry outlet. (Shalina's has been an almost yearly resource for our retreat gifts, providing us with cost-effective, theme-related items such as bookmarks, bracelets, chains, charms, and more. If you would like to contact them, call 214-630-6792, or write: Shalina's, 2629 North Stemmons Freeway, Suite 220, Dallas, TX 75207.)

Drama and "Interrupts"

Homecoming Session One Script

Background: For this retreat, we pretended that we were all gathered as alumnae returning to our high school. The retreat coordinator played the role of the school principal. We used every possible pun on *cow* we could think of. It really makes all the skits funnier if they are done with straight faces, as though having a cow as your school mascot is just an ordinary thing. The student council is referred to as the "student cowncil;" cheerleaders become "cowleaders."

There has been an emergency at the school, and a substitute cowleader has stepped in. She begins the weekend totally out of place with the snooty regular cowleaders but by the end of the weekend has won over everyone's hearts and turns out to do a pretty mean cartwheel! All the uniforms were done in black and white, incorporating cow print fabric.

The entire group of women attending the retreat was divided up into four teams with Team Leaders (called **Head Heifers**) selected before the retreat and informed of their responsibilities. The four groups were the Cow Belles (drill team), the Cow Patties (pep squad), the Bovine Band (school band), and the Student Cowncil (student council). There was also the school mascot, Mooreen, who led the Student Cowncil group. Mooreen was in full cow costume, including padding and udders. We also purchased props for each team as well as different colored cotton tank tops that could be worn over their regular clothes for group activities. The Cow Belles had handheld cowbells to ring. The Cow Patties had small black and white pom-poms. The Bovine Band had kazoos, and the Student Cowncil had small plastic megaphones. We called our small groups "Home Rooms," and our notebook, a "Yearbook."

EMCEE: As principal of this fine school, I want to welcome all of you to our Homecoming Weekend. We are so glad you are all here. To welcome our alumnae this weekend, we have many exciting events planned for you, including the selection of our Homecoming Dairy Queen. This year's senior class has been hard at work preparing many surprises for you, and at this time I would like to introduce the president of the Student Cowncil to kick off our Homecoming festivities. Please welcome our president! *[start applause, nothing happens]* Well, we seem to have a slight problem. Would the president of the Student Cowncil please come forward so we can get started? *[start applause again, nothing happens]* What is going on?

VICKI: *[sitting in the crowd, gets up, and begins to make her way forward to podium]* Excuse me, Principal. Excuse me, excuse me, sorry *[as she bumps and falls over people]*.

EMCEE: What is going on? Where's the president?

VICKI: *[pushes Emcee aside and takes over mic]* Excuse me, could I have your attention please! *[pounds gavel]* There has been a slight change of plans due to unforeseen circumstances; but don't worry, I am here to take over!

EMCEE: Who are you, and what do you think you're doing?

VICKI: I am the *vice* president of the Student Cowncil, and I am here to get this homecoming weekend under way!

EMCEE: Where's the president of the Cowncil? You can't just walk in here and take over! We have a full weekend of events planned, and I need the Homecoming Committee here to run things.

VICKI: Well, there's been a slight problem. We've had to make some emergency substitutions. But don't worry—everything will be great—if I could just have a little Cow Spirit up here to help me.

SOUND TECH: *[Start spirited, upbeat music such as "Jock Jams"; stop once Cowleaders have reached stage and stopped cheering and jumping.]*

[Cowleaders and Mascot Mooreen enter from back to music with pom-poms, throwing candy, running up to stage, and cheering.]

EMCEE: Wait a minute—Muffy and Buffy I recognize from our award-winning Cowleader squad. But who is that? *[pointing at Agnes]*

VICKI: Well, according to the official bylaws of the Student Cowncil manual, one alternate Cowleader is selected each year in case of emergency. *[Agnes jumps and cheers wildly.]*

EMCEE: Come over here, you! *[pointing at Agnes]* This must be some kind of emergency for you to become a Cowleader. Have you ever cheered before?

AGNES: No. *[looking downcast]*

MUFFY: We don't even want her on the Cowleader squad!

BUFFY: She's not one of us!

MUFFY: Look, she's painted over Huffy's name on her megaphone. Her name's Angus!

BUFFY: We can't be Muffy, Buffy, and *Angus!* We'll be laughed right off the stage at nationals!

EMCEE: Is your name really *Angus?*

AGNES: No, I just got so excited I spelled it wrong on my megaphone! It's Agnes!

VICKI: Look, it says right here in the Student *Cow*ncil manual: "An alternate Cowleader is allowed in case of emergency."

EMCEE: What is this emergency that you keep talking about?

VICKI, AGNES: Bovine Spongiform Encephalopothy!

EMCEE, MUFFY, BUFFY: What?

VICKI, AGNES: Bovine Spongiform Encephalopothy!

AGNES: You know, Mad Cow Disease! *[aside to crowd]* Look, we know we have already offended half of you by calling you cows. Now I figured I'd go ahead and offend the rest of you by making fun of a very serious disease.

EMCEE: You're going to milk this for all it's worth, aren't you!

VICKI: Last week the school cafeteria had a slight problem with the hamburgers they served, and most of the senior class has come down with Bovine Spongiform Encephalopothy.

BUFFY: Including the rest of our award-winning Cowleader squad!

MUFFY: And we were just getting ready for nationals!

BUFFY, MUFFY: What are we going to do? *[They start pouting and crying.]*

AGNES: Don't worry, fellow Cowleaders! I am here to save the day! *[performs cheer badly]* I've got spirit, yes I do! Line 'em up— milk 'em down—moo moo moo! *[hand motions milking a cow]*

MUFFY: There's no way we're working with her! Let's go Buffy! *[Muffy and Buffy stomp off stage]*

VICKI: Don't worry, Principal. I've got it all under control.

EMCEE: Whatever! *[goes and sits down]*

VICKI: If I could have your attention, please, I would like to introduce the emergency substitutions for Homecoming Weekend.

SOUND TECH: *[Start music, play until all team leaders are at front.]*

[Head Heifers march in from different corners of room.]

VICKI: Let me introduce _____ *[name of group leader]*, the second lieutenant of our drill team, the Cow Belles!

COW BELLES
GROUP LEADER: *[marches to front and bows]* Cow do you do?

VICKI: _____ *[name of group leader]*, the captain-elect of the pep squad, the Cow Patties!

COW PATTIES
GROUP LEADER: *[runs to stage and cheers wildly]* Go Cows!

VICKI: And _____ *[name of group leader],* the drum minor of our *cow*nty-renowned Bovine Band!

BOVINE BAND
GROUP LEADER: *[marches to stage with cow baton]* Mooooo!

VICKI: And don't forget, the head of the Student *Cow*ncil and our alternate school mascot—Mooreen! *[Mooreen bows and waves at crowd.]*

AGNES: Okay all you cows! Because of this emergency, we are all going to have to pull together. You are going to be divided up into four herds for the weekend according to your homeroom number. So look in your yearbook and find your homeroom number. If you are in homeroom number 1 through 8, stand up—you are a proud member of the Cow Belles!

COW BELLES
GROUP LEADER: Cow Belles! Moooooo!

AGNES: Okay, sit down. Now, if you are in homeroom number 9 through 16, stand up—you are a proud member of the Cow Patties!

COW PATTIES
GROUP LEADER: Cow Patties are the best!

AGNES: Okay, sit down. If you are in homeroom number 17 through 24, stand up—you are our Bovine Band!

BOVINE BAND
GROUP LEADER: *[Waves baton and cheers.]*

AGNES: Bovine Band, please take your seats. If you are in homeroom number 25 through 32, stand up—you are the newly elected representatives of the Student Cowncil!

MOOREEN: Student Cowncil rules!

AGNES: These are our four herds of cows and the Head Heifers for

Homecoming Weekend. If we all pull together, this will be the best homecoming ever! Now—just to get all you alumnae better acquainted—find two people you do not know, tell them where you went to high school, and what your school mascot was. *Go!*

SOUND TECH: *[Play Beach Boys song, "Be True to Your School."]*

AGNES: And now to get our first homecoming session started, here's our M.C., which stands for Moo Cow!

Introduction to Pep Rally and Bonfire Script

If you have a pep rally and bonfire on Friday night, use this script to introduce these events.

EMCEE: Now that we have finished homeroom, that will end our evening. I'm sure you are all really tired and just want to go to bed.

SOUND TECH: *[Play spirited music to get the audience's attention.]*

EMCEE: Oh no! I have just about had it with these interruptions. When is it going to end?

[Cowleaders and Mooreen run in cheering.]

AGNES: Excuse us, Principal _____, you didn't think the night was over, did you? We're just getting started!

MUFFY: Just herd yourselves right on out of this room!

MOOREEN: And get ready to moooove on to the Homecoming bonfire!

AGNES: Head 'em out!

EMCEE: And, ladies, you never know what kind of surprise we will have waiting for you! Let's go!

SOUND TECH: *[Play "Rawhide"—keep playing over and over until all have left the room.]*

Homecoming Session Two Script

EMCEE: Welcome, everyone! Please settle into your seats and get ready for a great morning session. *[Emcee reviews the previous evening's events.]* Wasn't that a great bonfire last night? I haven't had s'mores in years. I hope you all enjoyed the fun last night, but now it's time to start our session.

SOUND TECH: *[Start spirited music; stop once Cowleaders have reached stage and stopped cheering and jumping.]*

[Cowleaders and Mascot Mooreen enter from back to music with pom-poms, throwing candy, running up to stage, and cheering. Agnes has slightly improved her appearance and cheering ability.]

EMCEE: Oh no! Not again! I thought we had enough of you last night!

MUFFY: We have been trying to get rid of Angus, but she just keeps following us around!

BUFFY: She is never going to have what it takes to be a real Cowleader!

AGNES: I've really been practicing. *Please* just give me a chance!

EMCEE: Now girls, you have to make the best of this terrible situation.

MUFFY: All right, let's give it a try. Okay you cows! Let's hear some spirit—*cow spirit!*

BUFFY: Ready—Okay!

[Cowleaders do typical cheer, and Agnes goofs up.]

MUFFY: This is impossible!

BUFFY: You're ruining everything!

[Muffy and Buffy stomp off in disgust; Mooreen comforts Agnes.]

MOOREEN: Don't cry, Angus! Don't let them rain on your parade.

AGNES: Hmm . . . parade. What a great idea! To start things off for the big Homecoming game this afternoon, let's have a Homecoming Parade!

MOOREEN: That'll show 'em! You really do have cow spirit!

AGNES: Attention all you Cow Belles! Cow Patties! Student Cowncil, and Bovine Band! At 3 P.M. this afternoon, make your way down toward the front gate, then we'll divide up into our four herds and parade up to the playing field!

MOOREEN: Don't be a party cow-pooper! All you cows show up at three for the parade!

AGNES AND
MOOREEN: We've got spirit! Yes we do! Cow Spirit! *[then run out]*

SOUND TECH: *[Play Cowleader music until they leave room.]*

Homecoming Session Three Script

The Emcee opens session 3. She is interrupted by Cowleaders coming in through the back door.

SOUND TECH: *[Play Cowleader music until Cowleaders reach stage and stop cheering.]*

AGNES: Excuse me, Principal. We have an announcement.

EMCEE: Oh no! Not again! *[throws hands up in disgust and leaves stage]*

AGNES: I don't think she's going to make Homecoming Queen with that attitude!

MUFFY: One of the most exciting parts of our Homecoming weekend is coming up tonight!

BUFFY: Just because we won the big game this afternoon, don't think the fun's over!

AGNES: After homeroom, come back up here to the school auditorium for some special Homecoming entertainment!

MOOREEN: We're gonna party until the cows come home!

[All cheer, then run out.]

SOUND TECH: *[Play Cowleader music until they leave room.]*

Special Events

Bonfire and Hayride (suggested Friday night)

Bonfires and hayrides will resurrect fond memories for many participants. Most camps provide a designated place for a bonfire and may actually build it for you. Break out the marshmallows, or add chocolate and graham crackers to make s'mores.

Homecoming Parade (suggested Saturday afternoon)

In the first session, the participants were divided into teams: Cow Belles, Cow Patties, Bovine Band, and Student Cowncil. Designate on the campgrounds a time and place for each group to assemble, then have the Cowleaders lead the parade, marching to spirited music (using portable PA system or boom boxes). The Band should be tooting their kazoos, the Patties shaking their pom-poms, the Belles ringing their cowbells, and the Student Cowncil yelling through their megaphones. Your destination could be the dining hall or a softball game, any special group event.

Homecoming Dance (suggested Saturday night)

After small group Saturday evening, we all moved to the outdoor gym for a festive Homecoming Dance, complete with the Homecoming court nominees and the honorary Homecoming Dairy Queen. We gave each nominee a ribbon sash and crowned the queen during the dance. The decorations were simple— just white pillars with fabric draped on them—and the basketball goal was covered with a foam core cut-out of the happy cow like the ones we had all over camp. Our hospitality committee had popcorn, cookies, and other fun snacks to munch on. Our women *love* to dance. At least every other year we have a dance of some kind. They line dance, twist, bump, pony, and jitterbug the night away. Included below is a list of music used for the Homecoming Dance.

Homecoming Dance

AGNES: Welcome to our Homecoming Dance Through the Years! We have alumnae here from the forties, fifties, sixties, seventies, eighties, and nineties, and we have music for all of you. So, come on you Cows, get out there and dance!

Suggested Music

"1000 Dances"
"At the Hop"
"Bunny Hop"
"Catch a Wave"
"Cotton Eyed Joe"
"Dance to the Music"
"Good Vibrations"
"Hippy Hippy Shake"
"Hokey Pokey"
"I Want to Hold Your Hand"
"In the Mood"
"Limbo"
"Locomotion"
"Lord of the Dance"
"Rock Around the Clock"
"Shout"
"Stayin' Alive"
"Swim"
"The Chicken Dance"
"Time of Your Life"
"Twist"
"Twist and Shout"
"YMCA"

Chapter 10

The Cruise

Noah's Ark

*M*um's the word on this theme. Most women dream of a cruise vacation, so we billed this retreat as a cruise on the *S. S. Tarara* (which is *Ararat* spelled backward). Mount Ararat is the mountain in Turkey where Noah's ark supposedly rested. Everyone on the committee kept the theme a secret. Decorations were constructed in closed garages. Not until the doors to the first session were opened did the women learn the spiritual meaning of the theme—Noah's ark.

Design your publicity to resemble a luring cruise brochure. Decorate the campsite with life preservers and nautical memorabilia. We constructed the bow of a 24-foot cruiser out of wood and borrowed ship railings from a local decorating company. Everything outside gave the impression the weekend would be tossing on the high seas. But when the doors opened the first evening, the women entered into the belly of the ark, complete with wooden stalls of pairs of wild animals.

Since we desired to do a Noah's ark theme, we asked the teacher to speak on the life of Noah. The drama and interrupts played off the idea of Loretta Noah and her three daughters-in-law, who thought they were going on a cruise. The nautical setting was fun and easy.

For the evening activity we transformed the camp's picnic area into a seaport marketplace. Twinkle lights and Caribbean music helped set a festive atmosphere. The women pretended to disembark at a port-of-call and visit booths that had all sorts of fun giveaways that we had collected all year. Simple things like beads, sunglasses, travel size shampoos, and more were set up at picnic table booths. Passengers received a canvas retreat bag and were let loose to play. Our hospitality coordinator displayed an elaborate spread of snacks worthy of a five-star ocean liner.

Decorations

In each area except the main meeting room (which was the inside of the ark), we carried out the cruise theme. Life preservers, steam stacks, sea birds, anchors, and other nautical items made the place come alive. Our team constructed the cruise liner outside from 3 by 7-foot flats attached together and painted *S. S. TARARA* on the side. This became the favorite photo op for the weekend.

As the women walked into the belly of the ark in the main meeting room, they found themselves among pairs of life-size hippos, giraffes, cougars, turtles, birds, sheep, and other wild animals. We created these creatures from buckets, paper tubes, seemingly millions of miles of masking tape, and crunched up newspaper, then painted or covered them with fabric to look real. Split railings, artificial hay bales, and a large tree made the animals look right at home.

So how do you make a hippo? A giraffe? First we researched the basic skeletal structure of a particular animal. Then from buckets, paper tubes, and anything else that resembles that shape, we began taping, stapling, and stuffing whatever necessary to form that structure. After that we crumpled up newspaper to fill out the shape and wrapped the structure entirely in masking tape to give a smooth skin appearance. Ears, tails, and noses were also made from newspaper or cardboard, wrapped in masking tape, and attached however possible. When you are satisfied with the animal's structure, spray it with a primer. You can then paint it or find animal print fabric and glue it on. As you can see, there was no real science to this, so just enlist one of your creative ladies who will play with it and bring it to life.[1]

Throughout the weekend we added visual illustrations to complement the teacher's message. For instance, we added a 3-foot dove sitting on an olive branch, a balloon arch in rainbow colors, and a "stone" altar (also made from newspaper crumpled in balls, glued together, and painted). During Communion the women placed their commitment cards to the Lord on the altar.

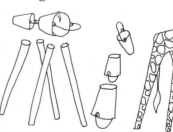

Though this retreat was rather elaborate and very fun to do, you could simplify the same theme using stuffed animals or flat wooden cut-outs of animals. Tweak it and make it work for you. Just enjoy!

Suggested Activity Schedule

Friday: **Session One**
                 Caribbean marketplace
Saturday: **Session Two**
                 free time and breakout sessions
                 Session Three
                 talent show
Sunday: **Session Four**
                 worship service

Publicity Logo

Protect the secrecy of your theme in your publicity. This adds to the drama and fun. Our logo pictured the bow of a ship and looked like a cruise brochure. We teased the women by placing a rainbow in the background, but no one understood its significance until we revealed the theme at the retreat.

Special Gift Ideas

In keeping with the biblical theme, you may choose to buy small, stained-glass rainbow sun catchers or silver chains with a Noah's ark charm. We also created our own rainbow bookmark.

Cut plastic or cardboard into a 1 by 3-inch rectangle and punch a hole for each colored ribbon. Cut different colored ⅛-inch satin ribbons into 18-inch strips. Fold ribbon in half; pull it through holes so that it forms a double strand of each color, then loop one end through the other, forming a cow-hitch or lark's head knot. Place the rectangle in the spine of your Bible and use the ribbon as bookmarks.

Drama and "Interrupts"

Scripts for this retreat theme are performed by the emcee, and Loretta Noah (Noah's wife) and her daughters-in-law, Mrs. Shem, Mrs. Ham, and Mrs. Japheth.

Noah's Ark Session One Script

SOUND TECH: *[Play tape of "Sea Cruise" and then switch to jungle/animal sound effects tape while people are entering.]*

EMCEE: What in the world is going on? What are all these animals doing in here? I don't get it! *Loretta!*

SOUND TECH: *[Start "Titanic" theme song—stop music once characters get on stage and settled.]*

[Loretta and three daughters-in-law enter from back in wind suits; Mrs. Shem and Mrs. Ham are struggling to carry a trunk.]

LORETTA: Hi, Captain *[Emcee's name]!* Isn't this exciting! We're almost ready to ship out!

MRS. SHEM: *Mother!* It's not ship out, it's cast off!

LORETTA: Whatever you say, honey—cast off, ship out. Let's go!

MRS. HAM, MRS. JAPHETH: *[carrying trunk and dropping it on stage]* This is sooooo heavy!

MRS. HAM: What all do you have in here?

LORETTA: Oh, nothing much, sweetie.

EMCEE: Wait a minute! What's going on here?

MRS. JAPHETH: *Mother!* That cheetah is looking at me funny!

EMCEE: What are all these animals doing here?

LORETTA: Aren't they just precious?

EMCEE: Okay. Stop. Where are we?

LORETTA: We're on the maiden voyage of the *S. S. Tarara*! The most popular cruise ship at _____ Church!

EMCEE: Well, this doesn't look like any cruise ship I've ever seen. I don't understand what all these animals are doing on board!

MRS. JAPHETH: *Mother!* I think that cheetah is moving closer!

EMCEE: Loretta! This is a zoo in here! We are supposed to all be going on a three-day cruise on a luxurious cruise ship.

LORETTA: Oh, don't worry, Captain _____! You are in for the time of your life!

EMCEE: That's what I'm afraid of!

MRS. SHEM: Mother! Her stateroom is bigger than mine!

MRS. HAM: It may be bigger, but at least your room isn't next to the elephants! Whew! The smell!

MRS. JAPHETH: We're right by the chicken coop—5 A.M.—cock-a-doodle-doo!

LORETTA: Girls! I told you we all have to get along. We may be here together for quite a while.

EMCEE: Quite a while? Wait a minute . . . oh no . . . don't tell me . . . this ship looks familiar—kind of like . . . an ark! Can we possibly be on an ark?

LORETTA: Ark—boat—cruise ship—what's the difference? I'm so glad you are all here!

MRS. SHEM: Mother! She says it's my turn to feed the animals—but I did it this morning. It's not fair!

LORETTA: Girls! Enough of this bickering. You get it together right now or I will have to call your father—and you know how busy he is!

EMCEE: Oh no! Don't tell me—the father you are referring to— would his name happen to be Noah?

LORETTA: Of course—do you know him? Isn't he just the cutest thing?

EMCEE: And that would make you . . .

LORETTA: Loretta Noah, of course. And these are my precious daughters-in-law: Mrs. Ham, Mrs. Shem, and Mrs. Japheth.

EMCEE: I don't believe this! Somehow we have gone back in time and landed on Noah's ark! I thought you told me this was the *S. S. Tarara!*

MRS. SHEM: Mother! Your dyslexia is acting up again. *[goes and turns the Tarara sign around to say Ararat]*

LORETTA: Oh, how silly, my mistake! Of course it's *Ararat.* That's what Noah told me our final destination would be!

EMCEE: Unbelievable! We have invited all these women to join us on a luxurious cruise ship, and now you tell me we're on the ark!

LORETTA: Isn't this great! We are going to have the best time! When Noah first told me about this trip, I didn't believe him. You know men. He's getting on a little in age. Close to his six-hundredth birthday.

EMCEE: Six hundred?

LORETTA: I'll never forget that midlife crisis he had at three hundred. I thought we'd never get through that. So when he told me about God telling him to build a big boat and prepare for a long voyage—well—there was no way I was going without all of you!

EMCEE: Does he know we're all here?

LORETTA: He said the passengers were coming two by two. So I invited two of my best friends, and they invited two of their best friends, and they invited two, and here we are!

MRS. HAM: *Mother!* What's in this big trunk? *[three daughters start opening trunk]*

LORETTA: Just the bare necessities.

EMCEE: Oh brother! I can't wait to see this!

LORETTA: Okay girls—let's get ready to sail! *[Girls start pulling out different things, including Dramamine patches.]* Slap those on behind your ear—that's supposed to keep us from getting seasick!

EMCEE: I think I'm starting to feel a little sick myself!

[Girls pull out more items.]

LORETTA: Tennis anyone? Golf club—ready for the putt putt course! Fanny packs strapped on!

MRS. SHEM: Mother! This looks funny. *[puts fanny pack on backward]*

MRS. HAM: You silly—a fanny pack goes in the front, not *on* your fanny!

LORETTA: Sunglasses! *[all put big sunglasses on]* Ready for the pool? *[snorkels, fins, beach towels over shoulders]*

MRS. JAPHETH: Mother, you know I burn when I get too much sun!

LORETTA: Don't worry, precious, I've thought of everything! *[Mrs. Ham pulls out big bottle of sunscreen and puts umbrella hat on Mrs. Japheth.]*

MRS. SHEM: Mother! Mrs. Japheth has an umbrella hat and I don't! *[Mrs. Ham takes umbrella hat off Mrs. Japheth and puts on Mrs. Shem. Mrs. Shem sticks tongue out at Mrs. Japheth.]*

EMCEE: What about bathing suits? This I've gotta see!

LORETTA: Of course we have bathing suits! Girls—*[they pull out four different suits—old fashioned, old lady type with skirt, tank, and bikini]*

EMCEE: Okay—let me guess—that one's yours. *[pointing to old fashioned suit]*

LORETTA: Of course not—*this* one's mine. *[grabs bikini and holds it up]*

EMCEE: Remind me to steer clear of the pool!

LORETTA: Oh, you're such a kidder! Almost ready! Mrs. Shem—got the camera?

[Mrs. Shem pulls out stone slab and chisel.]

MRS. SHEM: Say "cheetah"—and hold that pose! *[begins to chisel]*

LORETTA: We don't have time for this now. We're about to pull away from the pier! Get ready everyone—*bon voyage*—here we go!

SOUND TECH: *[Play thunder and lightning sound effects.]*

LORETTA AND
GIRLS: For heaven's sake! What's that noise?

EMCEE: I hate to tell you this—but you might be in for some stormy weather.

LORETTA: Oh, I almost forgot, Noah said we might see a few sprinkles—*girls!*

[All pull out parasols and open them over their heads.]

LORETTA: *Tarara* for now! We're off to the pool!

EMCEE: Thank you, Loretta and girls! I think we are in for a *very* interesting voyage!

SOUND TECH: *[Start up "Titanic" music again.]*

[Loretta and girls exit.]

Noah's Ark Session Two Script

SOUND TECH: *[Play Jars of Clay song "Flood" from the CD titled "Jars of Clay."]*

[Loretta and daughters-in-law come in wearing yellow slickers and rain gear.]

EMCEE: Oh my goodness! You girls look like something the cats dragged in!

LORETTA: Don't start messin' with me, *[Emcee's name]*. In all my four hundred plus years, I've never seen weather like this!

MRS. SHEM: Mother! I thought you said it was just supposed to sprinkle!

MRS. HAM: My hair is getting all frizzy!

MRS. JAPHETH: Five A.M. this morning—cock-a-doodle-do! Cock-a-doodle-do!

LORETTA: Now, girls, no reason to get snippy. We all have to get along. We've only been here one day and one night, and you are already fighting.

EMCEE: *[aside to audience]* I have a feeling if they knew it was going to be forty days and forty nights of rain, they'd jump ship right now!

LORETTA: Forty days and forty nights! You have got to be kidding! Why, that might sound something like this *[each character leads part of the audience in a different sound effect]*: first group—rub hands together; second group—make "clock" sounds with tongue; third group—pat knees gently; fourth group—pat knees harder; fifth group—stomp your feet. *[Once all the groups are going, it really does sound like a thunderstorm!]*

Well, I just wanted to let you know that even though the weather is not cooperating, Noah is at the wheel, and we are on course for a great day!

MRS. SHEM: Mother! Mrs. Japheth took my tennis racket and won't give it back!

MRS. JAPHETH: I did not! I took your umbrella hat! Oops—*[realizes she let out secret.]*

LORETTA: Girls! There will be plenty of free time this afternoon, and all shipboard activities will go on as planned, including horseback riding, tennis, volleyball, putt putt, archery, Creative Memories, napping competition, and much more!

MRS. SHEM: Something you might not be aware of: we will have skeet shooting off the rear of the ship. Be sure to aim at the clay pigeons—we can't afford to lose either of our real ones.

MRS. JAPHETH: There will also be a shuffleboard play-off this afternoon. If your puck goes overboard, don't worry. We have plenty of styles and sizes available to choose from—just check inside the elephant pen on the poop deck.

MRS. HAM: For those of you who need a little exercise after last night's midnight snack, join us on the Promenade Deck for a few fast laps with the cheetahs. Or, if you prefer a slower pace, take your time with the tortoises. But ladies, please watch your step!

MRS. SHEM: The bookmobile has also made a stop in dorm 1. Of course there is only one book available—Genesis, the serial. But it's by the number-one bestselling author (in fact, the only author), Moses.

LORETTA: So ladies, have a great afternoon! If you are looking for me, I'll be on the Verandah Deck taking on challengers in the deck chair rock-off!

Noah's Ark Session Three Script

This is an introduction to the entertainment.

SOUND TECH: *[Play Frank Sinatra CD, "New York, New York."]*

[Loretta and girls strut down the aisles all dressed up and waving at crowd.]

EMCEE: Loretta! I can't believe you're interrupting me again!

LORETTA: Hiya, sweetie! Ain't we lookin' fine!

EMCEE: Why are you all dressed up?

MRS. SHEM: *Mother!* Did you forget to tell them?

LORETTA: Oops—Did I forget to mention that we were all invited to sit at the captain's table tonight?

EMCEE: Yes, I'm afraid you forgot to mention that.

MRS. JAPHETH: *Mother!*

LORETTA: Oh well, I guess you will all just have to go back to your staterooms and change clothes!

EMCEE: Loretta—these women were told to come here and dress casually. They didn't bring fancy sparkle shoes and boas and rhinestones like you!

LORETTA: Well, then, they are just going to have to come up with something. I know, after small groups are over tonight, ya'll just run on back to your stateroom and put on all those beautiful souvenirs you picked up last night at the marketplace.

MRS. HAM: And don't forget those beautiful rainbow bracelets and rings!

LORETTA: Then hurry on back here for a night of shipboard entertainment you will never forget! *Tarara* for now!

SOUND TECH: *[Play just a few more lines of "New York, New York" as Loretta and girls exit.]*

Special Events

After small groups, everyone is welcomed back for some late night entertainment. Loretta and girls have reset the stage like a cruise ship lounge, complete with small skirted tables with candles. Several acts are presented with either an animal or cruise ship theme. Ideas include a group dance number performed with parasols to "Singin' in the Rain," a karaoke singer who has only performed in the "Lizard Lounge" to rave reviews, and a soloist performing "Don't Rain on My Parade."

Introduction to Caribbean Marketplace Script

Use this script to introduce the Caribbean marketplace we described for you earlier.

[Loretta goes through small groups and blows air horn calling them all back to the auditorium.]

LORETTA: Ladies! May I have your attention please! You might not have noticed, but we have actually been sailing along for over two hours!

No one's feeling seasick, are they? If you are, I have some extra Dramamine patches up here. Mine's working just great!

Well, just for fun, I've convinced Noah to make one quick stop so we can all do our favorite thing—*shopping!*

That's right! We've reached our first port-of-call and docked at the pier. And don't worry—you don't need any money—it's all duty free! So if you will just follow me—and let's do this in style. Come on everybody—let's conga!

SOUND TECH: *[Start Gloria Estefan's "Conga"—loudly!]*

[Loretta leads conga line out the door.]

Outside, booths were set up like a marketplace with games, shopping bags, carnival-type gifts, candy, bookmarks, popcorn, snacks, plastic sunglasses, and the retreat T-shirts. We also had frozen drink machines with tropical flavors.

A good source for inexpensive carnival-type gifts is Oriental Trading Company. Browse their store at www.orientaltrading.com or call 1-800-875-8480 to request a catalog.

Chapter 11

Lord and Ladies

The retreat team was enjoying the crisp chill of an October morning at Linda's lake house. But they were not there to rest. They were sequestered for the day, intent on creating a theme for the spring retreat. Once the theme was established, each one could begin brainstorming with her committee. Although the retreat was six months away, they were already excited and anxious to begin.

They gathered in the large den of overstuffed chairs and sofas with piping hot mugs of hazelnut coffee. After thanking God for this opportunity and petitioning for inspiration, they began the process. The speaker read through ideas she had already gathered as she prepared.

One of her illustrations was set in a castle. Suddenly one of the women spoke up, "Wouldn't it be great to do a medieval theme? Don't you just love all the cool things that go with that era? There are jousters and lords and ladies and knights in shining armor." Women with mental wheels turning began to dialogue about the concept. They spouted ideas as the energy germinated.

"What would we call it?" asked one woman.

"How about Lords and Ladies?" suggested another.

"No," piped up the worship leader, "how about *Lord* and Ladies? After all, isn't the focus going to be on our Lord?"

The room exploded with delight and the theme was born—a theme that would foster fun as well as a serious focus on the Lord of Lords. Linda challenged the team to "think castle" over the next six months as they prepared their respective aspects of the retreat.

Decorations

Full Stage Castle Backdrop

To create our medieval theme, we constructed a castle from lightweight Styrofoam. Take the measurements of your stage and graph out what you want your castle to look like. Keep in mind your room size. Don't overwhelm the room with something that is too big and overbearing, or so small that from the back it loses its effect. Fortunately for us we were aware that the camp had 2 by 4-foot Styrofoam cubes in their warehouse that they allowed us to take and re-paint to form our castle.

Our castle was 34 feet wide and 10 feet tall. We formed turrets (round towers) on either end using the borrowed blocks and large sheets of Styrofoam. To create the dental mold look across the top of the castle we took ¾-inch thick insulation foam purchased at an area hardware store and cut it with a utility knife to form the effect we wanted. In the middle of the castle front we made two smaller turrets that formed a 3-foot opening for the castle door. Hanging between the turrets was a banner that said "Castle *[church name]*." Smaller banners hung from the two larger turrets on either end. These exhibited our church initials in deep purple, royal blue, crimson, and white—colors we used throughout the decorations. Your banners could show your church logo or something that you want to emphasize from the speaker's talks. The banners on the podium were smaller versions of those on the turrets. Let your imagination go and have fun creating those little touches that make the weekend that much more special.

Elaborate wall hangings that hung from the ceiling proclaimed the names of Jesus, eloquently written in all sorts of jewels and braids. For this, networking is key. Don't make anything that you can borrow. The banners were borrowed by one of our young moms from her parents' church. We return the favor whenever we can by storing what we produce and making it available to others.

We also made banners or flags to adorn the twenty-two flagpoles that lined the driveway of the camp. There was no real rhyme or reason to these—just primary-colored, inexpensive cotton fabric cut in different geometric designs and sewn together in rectangles to fit the camp's existing flag poles. This is a great job for some of the women in your church who are more homebound but want to help, or consider planning a sewing day at the church to enjoy the fellowship of doing this project together.

Candlelight Backdrop

To set a more reverent atmosphere on Sunday, we removed the castle and brought in white pillars and candles. We spaced the candles across the front with tulle and gold lamé draped between them. In front were tall candleholders made out of 6-inch diameter PVC pipe. A glass globe sat in the PVC to hold the candle. Across the front of the entire stage were 465 candles. Two-inch PVC pipes were mounted on 8-inch by 4-foot plywood boards. The PVC was cut in five different lengths and then uniformly distributed on the boards. Glass votives sat in the pipe with votive candles in them.

This scene change set a very quiet atmosphere for that final time of worship, time around the Word, and Communion. We have used variations of this over the years for our Sunday service. The simplicity of lighting a few candles (keep in mind camp policies) in a smaller setting will do the same. We always serve Communion on Sunday morning. This is a great time to have one of your women's ministry staff or the pastor's wife lead.

Suggestions for Serving Communion

There are multiple ways to distribute Communion. For larger groups, we ask women leaders to stand at the front with baskets of bread and a chalice of juice or wine. (At IBC, the retreat committee serves Communion. Often the women comment on how much they appreciate being served by the hands that have worked to make the weekend such a special experience.) Women come up single file and dip the bread in the wine as they pass. This is a way to take Communion quickly. If you have a smaller group, you may want to pass the elements or ask the women to come up to the front to kneel. Make this special time an experience and a highlight of the weekend.

When serving a large group, assign women as ushers to help keep the ladies moving. Have a carefully thought-out plan of how that time should flow so that not a moment is wasted.

Suggested Activity Schedule

Friday: **Session One**
            Scarborough Fair

Saturday:	**Session Two**
	free time and breakout sessions
	Session Three
	Saturday Knight Life at the Castle
Sunday:	**Session Four**
	worship service

Publicity Logo

We found a beautiful photo of a medieval castle in the mist on the Internet and used it on the cover of the retreat notebook, posters around the church, brochure cover, and name and luggage tags. This misty piece of art created an air of excitement and anticipation as the time for the retreat approached.

Special Gifts

The medieval theme provides a wide variety of choices for special gifts. Purchase or create castle charms on a ribbon or wire to use as a bookmark. Write the Lord's Prayer in calligraphy and matte or frame simply. Decorative wall crosses also work well with the theme. Be creative—this topic can provide endless ideas.

Drama and "Interrupts"

Lord and Ladies Session One Script

Background: The main characters were Lady Gladys Parsley, the chatelaine of the castle; and her Three Ladies in Waiting: Lady Sage, Lady Rosemary, and Lady Thyme. We also had a Court Jester and a Town Crier in addition to our emcee.

EMCEE: *[Welcome, introduce special guests.]* We are so glad all of you are here. We have a wonderful weekend planned for you. And so without further ado . . .

SOUND TECH: *[Play trumpet fanfare, ten seconds only.]*

TOWN CRIER: *[comes in from back and bangs frying pan]* Hear ye! Hear ye!

COURT JESTER: *[comes out from behind stage and holds ears]*
We can hear ye all right!
Are you going to do that all night?

TOWN CRIER: Lord and Ladies, draw nigh and give attention to this court.

COURT JESTER: What are you doing?
                  The Ladies are booing!

TOWN CRIER: I'm the town fryer!

COURT JESTER: No—not the fryer,
                  Your role is town *crier!*

TOWN CRIER: It is? Oh no! *[starts to cry]* What are you?

COURT JESTER: I'm the Court Jester;
                  My stage name is Esther.

EMCEE: Excuse me, what's going on? And what's up with her?

COURT JESTER: She thought she would fry,
                  But now she must cry.

COURT JESTER: *[to Town Crier]*
                  Get rid of the pan,
                  And try it again.

[Town Crier pulls out a trumpet and blows a blast.]

TOWN CRIER: It is my honor, my lady, to announce the
                  gracious chatelaine of Castle _____,
                  Lady Gladys.

EMCEE: Lady who? And who do you think you are,
                  interrupting me this way?

TOWN CRIER: Well, I'm the . . . *[starts to cry loudly]* I'm
                  the . . .

COURT JESTER: There she goes,
                  Take cover when she blows!

[Town Crier continues to cry.]

145

TOWN CRIER: I'm the town crier! *[Blows nose loudly in banner attached to trumpet.]*

EMCEE: Well, for heaven's sake. I didn't mean to upset her!

COURT JESTER: Oh, it doesn't take much at all to get her going!
If she doesn't stop soon, we'll have to start rowing!

EMCEE: What do we do?

TOWN CRIER: Just let me see if I can get through this without breaking down. *[sniffs and blows nose in banner]*

EMCEE: Oh please!

COURT JESTER: Careful, she's, like, totally sensitive!

TOWN CRIER: And now, ladies of the realm of our Lord, please welcome the gracious chatelaine of Castle _____, Lady Gladys!

EMCEE: What's a chatelaine?

COURT JESTER: No one really knows, but I think it's not as wide as a chate-street. *ba dum pah. [spoken]*

EMCEE: That's a really bad pun.

COURT JESTER: Trust me, it might be the first, but it won't be the last!
Just wait until you hear from the rest of our cast.

EMCEE: I have a feeling we are in for a really long weekend!

TOWN CRIER: Hear ye! Hear ye! And away we go!

SOUND TECH: *[Play regal processional music until main characters get to the front.]*

[Entrance of Lady Gladys and three Ladies in Waiting.]

LADY GLADYS: *[curtseys]* Good evening, my lady, and welcome to our humble home.

LADY SAGE: Good evening. Please allow me to be of service. *[curtseys]*

LADY ROSEMARY: Welcome, may I offer you some refreshment? *[curtseys]*

LADY THYME: Thank you for gracing us with your presence. *[curtseys]*

TOWN CRIER: *[crying]* Aren't they just the sweetest things?

EMCEE: Well, thank you for your hospitality and welcome, but who are you?

LADY GLADYS: I beg your pardon, my lady, please allow me to introduce myself. I am Lady Gladys, in charge of this humble castle.

COURT JESTER: Be it ever so humble, there's no place like castle!
Trying to make that one rhyme was a bit of a hassle!

LADY SAGE: And we are her three Ladies in Waiting.

LADY ROSEMARY: And waiting.

LADY THYME: And waiting!

COURT JESTER: They've been waiting, waiting, waiting,
And it gets so irritating, irritating, irritating!

LADY GLADYS: And it is our honor to welcome you to Castle _____.
All has been made ready for you and our guests.

EMCEE: Okay, now you are taking this castle thing a little too far. It's just a theme!

TOWN CRIER: Oh no, now you're going to ruin everything! *[crying loudly]*

COURT JESTER: Trust me, at this point, you better just go with it!

LADY GLADYS: We have been eagerly awaiting your arrival, and royal preparations have been made to meet your every request.

LADY SAGE: We've been waiting sooooooooo long for you to get here!

LADY ROSEMARY: We've been waiting sooooooooo long to welcome you!

LADY THYME: And now the waiting is over, and we can get started!

EMCEE: I have a feeling this whole thing is getting away from me!

LADY GLADYS: And now, Lord and Ladies . . .

LADY SAGE: It is with deepest pride . . .

LADY ROSEMARY: And greatest pleasure . . .

LADY THYME: That we welcome you to Castle _____ tonight.

COURT JESTER: Please draw near and lend an ear . . .

TOWN CRIER: As we proudly present . . . the Retreat Committee!

[Note: At this point, the Retreat Committee comes on the stage wearing medieval pointed hats with crepe paper streaming from the point on top. We had rewritten the words to a popular fairy tale castle-themed song that the whole committee performed, ending with a kick line. We even received a standing ovation! The retreat chairman then introduced each committee person with a brief explanation of her role in the retreat.]

Lord and Ladies Session Two Script

Background: The ladies have put together nominees and winners for medals awarded for the games held the previous night at Scarborough Fair (to be described later under "Special Events"). The medals are on ribbons like Olympic medals and are read one at a time. During Scarborough Fair, we asked the volunteers running the booths to make note of the women who made a big impression at the different events. Each category had several nominees and one winner. The final award is a good opportunity to really embarrass either your women's pastor or the retreat speaker or coordinator. Just make sure the person you choose is a really good sport.

EMCEE: What a wonderful evening last night! How did you like the Scarborough Fair? Some of you were jousting late into the night, and did you make it to the juggling booth? I had a great time. Well, hopefully you got some sleep last night and

are ready for a wonderful session this morning. So let's get
started . . .

SOUND TECH: *[Trumpet fanfare, ten seconds only.]*

TOWN CRIER: *[comes out onto turret and blows trumpet]* Hear ye! Hear ye!

EMCEE: Oh no! Here they come again!

COURT JESTER: I thought I heard you call—
And good morning to you all!

EMCEE: Good morning to you. I'm afraid to ask, but what do you
have in store for us today?

TOWN CRIER: Attention, please—please welcome once again, Lady Gladys
and the Spice Girls!

SOUND TECH: *[Play Olympic theme as Lady Gladys and three Ladies in
Waiting enter carrying gold medals in baskets.]*

COURT JESTER: Parsley, sage, rosemary, and thyme;
Scarborough Fair was simply sublime.

LADY GLADYS: Oh, I am so glad you enjoyed it!

LADY SAGE: We had such fun watching the jousting tournament!

LADY ROSEMARY: Why, you would think some of you had never jousted
before!

LADY THYME: And the javelin throw—how thrilling!

EMCEE: Some of you got a little vicious! It's a good thing those were
just beanbags!

TOWN CRIER: Are you going to give out prizes?

LADY GLADYS: Of course we are! Royal rewards for knights and ladies alike!

LADY SAGE: Oh, I just can't wait to reward the knight who wore my color.

LADY ROSEMARY: What color would that be?

LADY THYME: Sage green, of course!

COURT JESTER: Whether jousting or juggling or fighting with swords,
Come forward when called and claim your reward!

[Ladies take scrolls from baskets one at a time and read.]

- For the worst jugglers, the nominees are _____, _____, and _____, but the gold medallion goes to _____.
- For the ladies least likely to toss a beanbag anywhere near a dragon, the nominees are _____, _____, and _____, but the gold medallion goes to _____.
- For the jouster least likely to hit the target, the nominees are _____, _____, and _____, but the gold medallion goes to _____.
- For the ladies least likely to toss a javelin anywhere near a target, the nominees are _____, _____, and _____, but the gold medallion goes to _____.
- For the ladies least likely to sport a tattoo or have her face painted, the nominees are _____, _____, and _____, but the gold medallion goes to _____.

And now for our final award. This is an honorary medallion given to the worst all-around Scarborough Fair-goer: *[name of Pastor to Women or Director]*! Please come forward!

First of all, she refused to juggle more than one ball at a time; then she got stuck trying to climb over the fence to get to the checkerboard; she hit another woman with the cross-bow at archery; then she got mad and tossed someone out of the sword fight ring; she went to the sand art booth and ate all the sand candy; then she shinnied up the maypole; when she made it to beginner's jousting, she broke the tricycle; and, finally, she had a Harley Davidson tattooed someplace we can't mention!

Thanks, _____, for making all the rest of the competitors look so good!

LADY THYME: And now the waiting is over and all the medals have been presented.

TOWN CRIER: But I didn't win anything!

LADY GLADYS: You are such a crybaby! If I had known you were going to carry on so, I wouldn't have given you this role!

EMCEE: Well, thanks, Lady Gladys, Sage, Rosemary, and Thyme. Now can we please get on with our regular session?

LADY THYME: Pardon me, Lady Whoever You Are, but wouldn't you like to know the rest of the day's schedule?

TOWN CRIER: Oh no, now you've hurt *her* feelings!

LADY ROSEMARY: There are lots of activities planned for today, including a nature walk, scrapbooking, dominoes, and cards.

LADY THYME: I'm so tired from all the festivities last night, I think I will just go back to my turret room and take a nap!

COURT JESTER: You'll be spread out all around the castle
                Finding something to do won't be a hassle.

EMCEE: And don't we have something special planned for tonight?

TOWN CRIER: Hear ye! Hear ye! It is my great honor to announce "Saturday Knight Life at the Castle," a talent show presented for your pleasure.

LADY GLADYS: A talent show! How exciting! What will *we* be performing?

TOWN CRIER: Well, *we* had tryouts, and, unfortunately, *you* didn't make it.

LADY THYME: Didn't make it? That's impossible!

LADY ROSEMARY: We *are* the Spice Girls, you know!

LADY THYME: And we've been waiting, waiting, and waiting for a chance to perform!

COURT JESTER: The Spice Girls are nixed, the line-up's been fixed.
We're sorry, you're out—now just go and pout!

TOWN CRIER: Talk about a crybaby! You're not even spices. You're just herbs!

LADY GLADYS: As the royal chatelaine of this castle, I demand that you give us a chance to participate in the talent show.

TOWN CRIER: What kind of talents do you have? I'm not buying the Spice Girls bit.

LADY THYME: You'll just have to wait . . .

LADY ROSEMARY: And wait . . .

LADY THYME: And wait and see!

COURT JESTER: Who will win this debate? We'll all have to wait.
Will the Spice Girls perform, or get locked in their dorm?
One trick or two they might have up their sleeve
But the show must go on, not one of you leave!

SOUND TECH: *[Play processional music.]*

Lord and Ladies Session Three Script

This is an introduction to Saturday Knight Life at the Castle.

EMCEE: Welcome back, everyone. I hope you had a great afternoon. *[Talk about games, activities, etc.]* And we have a wonderful evening planned for you. Now let me see if I can sneak this one past them. Let's see if we can get started without any of those annoying interruptions.

SOUND TECH: *[Play trumpet fanfare, ten seconds only.]*

TOWN CRIER: *[comes out and blows trumpet]* Hear ye! Hear ye!

EMCEE: Oh no! I thought we had seen the last of you!

TOWN CRIER: *[crying]* You did? But I thought you were starting to like me!

EMCEE: Esther, come help me with her!

COURT JESTER: Don't worry, I'm here. There's nothing to fear!
Now you stop your crying, or again you'll be frying!

TOWN CRIER: *[sniff, sniff]* Okay, I think I can make it. Hear ye! Hear ye!
Please welcome Lady Gladys and her Ladies in Waiting,
waiting, and waiting!

SOUND TECH: *[Play processional music.]*

[Entrance of Lady Gladys and her three Ladies in Waiting.]

LADY GLADYS: Good evening once again, my lady. I trust you have had an
enjoyable day.

LADY THYME: We've been waiting all day to see you again!

LADY ROSEMARY: We've been waiting all day to audition for your talent show!

LADY THYME: And I know all of you have been waiting for us to perform!

EMCEE: *[to Town Crier]* I thought you had this handled. Isn't the
talent show set?

TOWN CRIER: Yes, it is, but I just don't know how to tell them. They will be
so disappointed! And it just makes me so sad!

COURT JESTER: You must do your job, and try not to sob,
If you don't make them go, they'll ruin the show!

LADY GLADYS: Must I remind you, my ladies, that I am in charge of this
castle, and I insist you let us perform!

LADY THYME: Come on, girls, let's show them what we've got!

EMCEE: *[to Town Crier]* Do something!

TOWN CRIER: I can't—they'll turn me back into the town fryer!

[Emcee throws up her hands in disgust and leaves stage.]

COURT JESTER: It's the worst of our fears, you might plug your ears,
I'm afraid that your cheers will soon turn to jeers!

TOWN CRIER: Hear ye! Hear ye! Introducing Gladys, Knights, and the Pips!

*[**Note**: We had several large standing suits of armor that we used for this routine. Lady Gladys also had a small knight that she held while she lip-synced the lyrics. The Ladies in Waiting lip-synced the back-up lyrics while performing "Pips" style routines to "Midnight Train to Georgia."]*

SOUND TECH: *[Play Gladys Knight and the Pips CD, "Midnight Train to Georgia," until Town Crier blows her trumpet and interrupts.]*

TOWN CRIER: Please stop! I just can't take it anymore! You aren't even really singing!

COURT JESTER: You must leave the stage, we're all in a rage,
Lip-syncing is awful, I'm sure it's unlawful.

LADY GLADYS: We now take our leave, but no one must grieve,
Of us you are ridding, but we simply were kidding.

LADY SAGE: Our time's at an end, but we'll see you again . . .

LADY ROSEMARY: At entertainment tonight, and it's sure to delight . . .

LADY THYME: We'll be right at the front, sitting next to our knight!

COURT JESTER: It's the end of their skit,
And they've been quite a hit.

TOWN CRIER: They must say good-bye, and I simply must cry.

COURT JESTER: So what else is new?

Special Events

Scarborough Fair (Friday night, after small groups)

The castle theme birthed an evening event of interactive medieval games and crafts to entertain. This became a time for women to "let their hair down" and have fun. We called the event Scarborough Fair and treated the women to booths of face painting and tricycle jousting.

Introduction to Scarborough Fair Script

EMCEE: Thank you for coming back. I hope you had a great time in your small groups. So unless there is something else . . .

SOUND TECH: *[Play trumpet fanfare, ten seconds only.]*

TOWN CRIER: *[comes out and blows trumpet]* Hear ye! Hear ye!

EMCEE: Oh no! Not again!

TOWN CRIER: Are you not glad to see me? *[starts to cry]*

EMCEE: Where's that court jester? Esther, please make her stop!

COURT JESTER: I've been trying, but she won't stop crying!

EMCEE: Well, what can we do? We have to do something to cheer her up.

COURT JESTER: Now dry your eyes, we have a surprise!

SOUND TECH: *[Play Simon and Garfunkel CD, "Scarborough Fair."]*

[Entrance of Lady Gladys and her three Ladies in Waiting. They are carrying baskets of fresh parsley and sticking sprigs of spices in their hair and on their costumes, asking each other, "Are you going?"]

LADY GLADYS: Good evening once again, my lady. Will you be attending the festivities tonight?

LADY SAGE: We just can't wait to get started!

LADY ROSEMARY: And we are all dressed up for the occasion!

LADY THYME: You must join us, my lady. You and all our guests.

EMCEE: What do you have cooked up for us now?

COURT JESTER: Fun is in the air, it's a Scarborough Fair!

LADY GLADYS: And you must try to guess our names!

COURT JESTER: How fun! It's a game—you must guess their name.

LADY GLADYS: These should give you a clue. *[points to parsley in hair]*

EMCEE: What is that—parsley?

LADY GLADYS: You've guessed—I am Lady Gladys *Parsley!*

LADY SAGE: And I'm Sage!

LADY ROSEMARY: My name is Rosemary!

LADY THYME: And I'm just in Thyme!

COURT JESTER: Better known as the Spice Girls! *[Girls strike a "Spice Girls" pose.]*

EMCEE: Oh no, another bad pun!

TOWN CRIER: Attention, ladies of the realm. Your presence is requested this evening at our Lord's Scarborough Fair.

LADY GLADYS: There will be games, face painting . . .

LADY THYME: Dragon fighting . . .

LADY ROSEMARY: A jousting tournament . . .

LADY THYME: And maybe even tattoos!

EMCEE: That sounds like fun! How do we get there?

LADY GLADYS: Just follow us as we wander up the lane to an acre of land . . .

LADY THYME: *[singing]* parsley, sage, rosemary, and thyme . . .

LADY ROSEMARY: Between the salt water and the sea strand . . .

LADY THYME: Enough singing! Let's just go!

COURT JESTER: So the question is, truth or dare: Are *you* going to Scarborough Fair?

LADY GLADYS: Parsley . . .

LADY THYME: Sage . . .

LADY ROSEMARY: Rosemary . . .

LADY THYME: and Thyme . . .

EMCEE: are sure to be there! This rhyming thing is contagious!

COURT JESTER: Now off you must go, and we'll meet you there,
For fun and a treat, it's Scarborough Fair!

SOUND TECH: *[Play Simon and Garfunkel, "Scarborough Fair."]*

Below you will find many ideas on how to decorate and staff possible activities and booths in the fair.

Setting

- yard torches
- flags
- twinkle lights

- booths
- tables
- strolling minstrel
- lots of candles

Suggested Prizes

- chocolate or gum coins
- beads
- bookmarks
- candy
- wands

Activities and Booths

Archery: Workers must make sure that everyone has a bow and the Nerf "arrows" to shoot at the target. A demonstration on how to use the bows and arrows should be given as needed. Allow three arrows per person. One person will be the arrow retriever, and one person will need to explain the rules (stand behind this line, shoot at this target, hold the bow like this, etc). Each participant that hits the target wins a prize.

- Supplies needed: plastic bows and Nerf arrows, targets, markers to show shooters where to stand

Juggling: Workers must entertain groups of women with their juggling and "teach" interested women how to juggle. Chairs will be set up for your audience.

- Supplies needed: demonstrators, table, objects to juggle (balls, oranges, beanbags, etc.)

Sword Fighting: Workers must time each match and make sure that those participating have an inflatable sword and shield. The winner will receive a prize! One helper will be the squire (holding swords and shields until ready), and one person will explain the rules and keep score. (Each match will last one minute. Points are scored by striking the body or head with the sword.)

- Supplies needed: inflatable swords, shields, jousting field marked off with ropes and poles

Maypole: Position each lady at the poles with a ribbon in her hand. Four ladies walk left, in time to music; four ladies walk inside them to the right, wrapping the pole with ribbon (or tying each other up!).

- Supplies needed: light poles, eight long strips of fabric or ribbon, music

Lawn Checkers: Divide ladies up into two sides. Each woman will be a checker and is outfitted in a colored vest to designate her team. Two women will be appointed to be the "players" who tell the checkers where to move. In the end, it becomes just a big game of human leapfrog!

- Supplies needed: lawn paint—create checkerboard on grass, vests in two colors to distinguish sides. Can be played with as few as four per team or as many as twelve. Two "players" to play the game.

Beanbag Toss: Give each lady three beanbags and line them up behind the starting line. They will then toss the bags and try to get them into the holes on the dragon (bucket with picture of dragon). Any woman getting a bag into a hole gets a prize. Each participant gets a ticket.

- Supplies needed: dragon board with holes, buckets, beanbags, markers for distance

Jousting: Workers must make sure that everyone has a steed (scooter or tricycle), a lance (water noodle), and a shield. Hold the shield and the handle of the scooter in the left hand and the lance in the right. Charge toward the target and either knock over the boxing bag or aim at and hit the ring with the lance. One person will need to demonstrate. Each participant that hits the target will get a prize.

- Supplies needed: scooters and/or tricycles, foam lances (water noodles), lane markers (cones), shields, targets—rings or blow-up clowns

Puppet Show: Entertain your audience with a short puppet show. Each show should last no more than five minutes. Set up chairs for the audience and schedule a two to three minute break between each show.

- Supplies needed: puppet stage, puppets, and puppeteer, chairs for audience

Stained Glass: Make sure each lady has a "stained glass" coloring page with a classical design (any medieval or religious theme), supply colored pencils, and sharpen them when needed.

- Supplies needed: coloring pages, colored pencils, pencil sharpeners

Candle Making: Teach the women how to make a candle using a wick, Crock-pots full of wax, and cool water for cooling the candles. Women will drop wicks alternately into wax and cool water to form candle.

- Supplies needed: candle booth, Crockpots, wax and wicks (restarted candles), pots of cool water

Princess Hats: Hand out starter hats and make sure there are plenty of decorations available to enhance them. Supply glue bottles and staples.

- Supplies needed: cone hats, decorations (glitter, sequins, lace, streamers, etc.), tissue paper, glue, and staples

Picture Spots: For use during the entire weekend, produce a medieval scene, large enough for women to pose behind, with the faces of characters cut out. Participants can photograph their friends for a fun souvenir.

- Supplies needed: 4 by 8-foot sheets of insulation foam, knight and fair maiden cutouts.

Face Painting: Recruit artists to paint simple designs on faces.

- Supplies needed: face paints, brushes, handheld mirrors

Tattoos: Recruit volunteers to adhere press-on tattoos to a range of body parts. Boundaries on where to place these tattoos may be necessary!

- Supplies needed: water, sponges, and press-on tattoos

Saturday Night Talent Show

We asked participants to connect their talent acts to the medieval idea. Below are their creative ideas that made the talent show another way to carry out the overall theme throughout the weekend.

Some tap-dancing older women choreographed and performed an Irish "Riverdance" routine. We also enjoyed watching one young lady display her clogging expertise.

Three different groups of young married women danced to "Queen of Hearts," "We Will Rock You," and "Dancin' Queen" in the spirit of the popular movie *A*

Knights Tale. "The Queenie Sister" sang a medley from all sorts of songs with references to knights, queens, and kings.

One group performed a skit—a take-off on the morning show *The View.* Starting in medieval times, one of the "hosts" went forward in a time machine to the present day and brought back items related to women. The discussion that followed had the crowd in stitches!

Don't be limited by these examples. Take the idea and run with it, giving your own women the opportunity to be creative, fun, and gifted.

Sample Retreat
Site Contract

Christian Camps
Route 1, Box 21
Detroit, Texas 75436-9700
903-674-3159

Jan-Kay Ranch Rental Contract

1. Organization Name: _____
   Address: _____
   Contact Person: _____ Phone: _____
   Home Address: _____ Title: _____

2. Camp Dates: _____
   Beginning: _____ Ending: _____
   First Meal: _____ Last Meal: _____

3. This contract is for ____ nights lodging and ____ meals at the cost of
   _____ per adult.

   Family Rates:
   Ages 15–up $_____; Ages 9–14 $_____; Ages 5–8 $_____;
   Ages 1–4 $_____; Under 1 $_____

4. The renting group agrees to pay a guaranteed minimum of $_____,
   regardless of the number of persons actually in attendance.

5. The renting group agrees to pay by check or cash the balance of the final bill prior to their departure from camp.

6. The renting group agrees to pay for damages to Jan-Kay Ranch's property (beyond that of normal wear and tear) caused by any members of their group.

7. It is understood that this retreat can be canceled up to ninety days prior to the opening day of camp with loss of deposit only. If cancellation is necessary after that time, the renting group agrees to pay the guaranteed minimum stated in item number 4.

8. The renting group agrees to comply faithfully with the policies listed on the reverse side of this contract.

9. The renting group realizes that there is an element of risk in activities it may participate in while staying at Jan-Kay Ranch. The renting group assumes full responsibility for its members for any accident or personal injury or property damage by or to a guest that may occur while staying at Jan-Kay Ranch. The renting group hereby releases, indemnifies, and holds harmless Jan-Kay Ranch, its agents and employees, from and against any and all claims, liabilities, suits, actions, damages, or losses. The renting group agrees to provide Jan-Kay Ranch with a "Certificate of Insurance" with this contract.

10. Please sign this contract and return with your $_____ deposit.

This contract shall be binding when a copy bearing the required signatures has been mailed to the renting organization.

Accepted by Jan-Kay Ranch: _____

Date: _____

Senior Pastor or C.E.O.: _____

Camp Representative Contact Person: _____

The Following Policies Are Considered Part of the Rental Contract

1. Serving arrangements for meals:
   a. Evening meals served upon arrival of a group are not scheduled later than 7 P.M.
   b. Meal times: Breakfast: 8 A.M.; Lunch: 12:30 P.M.; Supper: 6 P.M.
   c. Promptness to meals is essential to insure the food is at its best!
   d. Adherence to meal-time procedures is expected.
2. Children under eighteen years of age must stay in the room with their parents. The rental group and the child's parents are responsible for the supervision, safety, care, and well-being of any guests in their group.
3. Please turn in your registration forms, retreat schedule, and your exact count immediately upon your arrival at the campgrounds.
4. Full payment must be made for *all* guests who are in your group for any length of time. No reduction can be made for part-time campers.
5. No alcoholic beverages, unprescribed drugs, fireworks, firearms, paint ball guns, personal pets, or shaving cream (except for shaving) are allowed.
6. Please keep the campgrounds clean by keeping paper and litter picked up.
7. Safety rules for boating:
   a. All guests must wear a properly secured life vest.
   b. Parents must be present when their children under eighteen years of age are using the boats.
   c. No ramming or tipping of the boats and *no swimming in the lake.*
8. Help conserve energy! Turn off lights and air conditioning/heating when rooms and buildings are not in use. Keep outside doors and windows closed when heaters or air conditioners are in use.
9. Two lifeguards are to be provided by the rental group when its people are using the pool (Texas State Department of Health requirement). No suntan oils are allowed in the pool water. Bathing suits are to be worn in the pool area only. Modest swimwear is required. Observe pool rules!
10. Capacity of the hotel: 16 couples, 16 families, or 63 singles. Singles groups and groups that have more than 16 couples/families must enforce a standard that places men with men and women with women.
11. Accident/illness insurance information:
    a. Report all injuries to our camp staff immediately.
    b. We furnish an Excess Insurance Policy. There is a $25 deductible on outpatients and a $250 deductible on admitted patients. Policy maximum is $2,500 per accident or illness.
    c. Insurance will not cover injuries that occur while playing games in the dark!

12. Jan-Kay Ranch's Buffalo Hotel will furnish towels and linens but not maid service. Sheets will be folded on your bed when you arrive. When you leave, please return used linens and towels to the designated area.

13. Check in time is no earlier than two (2) hours before your first meal, or if arriving the night before, no earlier than 5 P.M.

14. Checkout time is no later than two (2) hours after the serving time of the last meal.

15. *No* smoking is allowed in any building! Ask for designated areas.

16. *Your activities must reflect Christian principles.*

Sample Registration Form

Annual Irving Bible Church Women's Retreat

Date: _____

Name: _____

Address: _____

City: _____ Zip: _____

Phone: (home) _____ (work) _____

E-mail: _____

❑ I would like to stay in a **Cabin**. (Each cabin will accommodate ten to fifteen per side) $100

   I would like to room with:

❑ I would like to stay in the **Lodge**. (Minimum four to a room. Two queen size beds) $100

   I would like to room with:

❑ I am providing a scholarship of: $_____

❑ For physical reasons, I would like to rent a **Golf Cart**. ($110 for weekend)

Please designate T-shirt size:
❑ S   ❑ M   ❑ L   ❑ XL   ❑ XXL   ❑ XXXL

❑ **Digital Photo**: (for those not registering in person, e-mail photo to
_____)

Contact [name of person in charge of registration] with any registration questions.

Registration Information

1. Please make checks payable to IBC denoting "Women's Retreat" in the memo field. Your check must be accompanied by the registration form in order to hold your place.
2. Registration deadline is March 10. Space is limited and registration is handled on a "first come, first served" basis, so register early.
3. IBC members may apply for scholarships by requesting the necessary form at the sign-up kiosk in the Town Square. *Availability is limited.*
4. No refunds can be issued after March 17, and cancellations prior to this are subject to a $25 cancellation fee.
5. All room requests will be honored on a "first come, first served" basis.
6. IBC Women's Retreat is open to all women 18 years or older. Sorry, we cannot accommodate infants (including nursing babies).

Lakeview Room Arrangements

• Cabins hold ten to fifteen on each side with a small sitting room in between and bath facilities. You will need to bring pillow, linens, blanket, and towels.
• Lodge has two queen beds and private bath. Towels and linens are provided. *Each room must hold four ladies.*

If you are interested in helping, please contact the appropriate committee member below:

Coordinator: _____

Fun and Games: _____

Entertainment: _____

Notebooks: _____

Snacks: _____

Registration: _____

Mini Sessions: _____

Worship: _____

Small Groups: _____

Prayer: _____

Photography: _____

Decorations: _____

Sample Scholarship Form

Irving Bible Church Women's Retreat Scholarship Form

Only those who are members or regular attendees are eligible for consideration for financial assistance for the IBC Women's Retreat.

Name: _____

Address: _____

City: _____ Zip: _____

Phone: (home) _____ (work) _____

E-mail: _____

❑ Married   ❑ Single   ❑ Divorced

Children's Names   Ages

_____   _____

_____   _____

_____   _____

_____   _____

How long have you been a member of or attended IBC?

Do your spouse and/or children attend IBC?

Have you received a scholarship to our women's retreat before?

Please provide a personal reference of someone attending IBC who has known you for at least three months.

Name: ——————————————— Phone Number: ————————————

Please list the IBC ministries in which you are currently involved (*not including Sunday worship attendance*):

Are there special circumstances we should consider as we review your request?

How much can you contribute toward your cost of the retreat?

Amount of scholarship requested:

_____

Applicant's Signature

If there is any additional information you would like us to consider, please note it on the back of this sheet!

Amount of scholarship awarded:

_____

Board Member's Signature

Sample Housing Confirmation Form

We are excited you are coming to the
Twenty-Third Annual IBC Women's Retreat!

Your housing will be:

Lodge: _____ Cabin: _____

(All those in cabins must bring twin size bedding and towels.)
(Lodge rooms that have more than four need to bring twin bedding and towels.)

When you check in:

Balance due of $_____

No check in before 3 p.m.

You must register at the Multipurpose Building to pick up key.

Room changes will be made by the approval of Linda Butcher only.

Questions about housing? Contact Linda at (e-mail address) or (phone number).

Other questions, contact Linda Robinson at (e-mail address) or (phone number).

Small Groups: You will be in a small group with the ladies you are rooming with. We will, however, provide alternative groups on request for those who would desire something different. These will be generic or specialized, that is, young singles, and so forth. Please contact one of the names below before March 23 to be assigned to one of these groups.

Shirley Hotchkiss: (e-mail address) or (phone number)

Bev Ridgway: (e-mail address) or (phone number)

Dinner begins at 6 P.M., and our first session begins at 7:30!

See you there!

Endnotes

Chapter 1: Define Your Purpose

1. Sue Edwards and Kelley Mathews, *New Doors in Ministry to Women: A Fresh Model for Transforming Your Church, Campus, or Mission Field* (Grand Rapids: Kregel, 2002).
2. Miriam Neff and Debra Klingsporn, *Shattering Our Assumptions: Who Is Today's Christian Woman* (Minneapolis: Bethany House, 1996), 194–95.
3. Elizabeth Baker, *How to Hang Loose in an Uptight World* (Gretna, La.: Pelican, 2002), 17.
4. Ibid., 101.
5. Ibid., 15.
6. Excerpted from Edwards and Mathews, *New Doors in Ministry to Women*, 152–56.

Chapter 3: People Behind the Scenes

1. Sue Edwards and Kelley Mathews, *New Doors in Ministry to Women* (Grand Rapids: Kregel, 2002), 58–90.

Chapter 5: Prepare Ahead

1. Sue Edwards and Kelley Mathews, *New Doors in Ministry to Women* (Grand Rapids: Kregel, 2002), 26.
2. Ibid., 26–38, 135–151.
3. Edith Schaeffer, *Hidden Art* (Wheaton: Tyndale House, 1979), 14.
4. Max Lucado, *In the Eye of the Storm* (Dallas: Word, 1991), 225.
5. Evelyn Underhill, *Worship* (London: Nisbet and Co., 1936), 61.

Chapter 10: The Cruise

1. For those interested in this project but feeling overwhelmed, you may consider contacting Linda personally. See page 16 for her consulting business contact information.